Holocaust Literature

Study Guides to 12 Stories of Courage

Kathleen Gagnon
and
Dianne Ruxton

WALCH PUBLISHING

User's Guide
to
Walch Reproducible Books

As part of our general effort to provide educational materials which are as practical and economical as possible, we have designated this publication a "reproducible book." The designation means that purchase of the book includes purchase of the right to limited reproduction of all pages on which this symbol appears:

Here is the basic Walch policy: We grant to individual purchasers of this book the right to make sufficient copies of reproducible pages for use by all students of a single teacher. This permission is limited to a single teacher, and does not apply to entire schools or school systems, so institutions purchasing the book should pass the permission on to a single teacher. Copying of the book or its parts for resale is prohibited.

Any questions regarding this policy or requests to purchase further reproduction rights should be addressed to:

Permissions Editor
J. Weston Walch, Publisher
P. O. Box 658
Portland, Maine 04104-0658

1   2   3   4   5   6   7   8   9   10

ISBN 0-8251-3271-1

Copyright © 1997
J. Weston Walch, Publisher
P. O. Box 658 • Portland, Maine 04104-0658

Printed in the United States of America

Contents

Overview

World War II provides one of the most important lessons in all of history. Not only did this war involve all parts of the globe, it also taught us a great deal about prejudice and persecution. We learned that barbarism is not limited to uncivilized society, but that it can subtly creep into even the most genteel society and seem justified.

History books have plenty to say about World War II, but as far as literature is concerned, the storytellers have been fairly silent. *Anne Frank: The Diary of a Young Girl* was the first and is probably the best-known piece of literature that has come out of this era. Perhaps it's because the people who were involved in World War II are getting older and the memories will soon be extinct that the survivors are finally telling their stories. The Holocaust literature genre has grown in the past 15 to 20 years to include stories from all over the world. They are remarkable stories of ordinary people who experienced the anguish firsthand, articulately expressing how they survived both physically and emotionally. It's important that people of all future generations learn from what happened to help ensure that nothing like it happens ever again.

There is enough Holocaust literature written and published today to provide stories that will appeal to every student in the classroom. This multibook unit offers choices that will appeal to each student, and then enables the class to bring all the different stories together so that the students can achieve a broader, more accurate, picture of World War II and its effects on our world.

The books included in this unit tell those stories. One story is told from the perspective of a Jewish prisoner in a Nazi concentration camp. Another is about a Hungarian teenager trying to survive the bombing of her city. There's also a German child forced to join the Hitler youth in order to survive the Nazi regime. One historical account tells of a young American girl who must move to an internment camp located in California because of her family's Japanese ancestry. Yet another story tells of a 15-year-old American boy who chooses to join the military illegally, thinking he can help to kill Hitler. These stories paint a global picture of the war, affording a personal and human view of World War II that history books alone cannot provide.

The main component we looked for in making our selections was human interest. From these books, students are able to see how young people their own age found the courage to survive the horrors that took place during a tumultuous era.

One of the objectives of this unit is to help students relate to the subject matter on a personal level. What does this whole experience mean to today's students and to future students? And what is there about the writers' experiences that the students have encountered before in some way? There are writing assignments for each story that encourage students to look inside themselves and clarify their own ideas and feelings about the war and about being a teenager.

Writing is very important in this unit on an individual level, but we have found that group work helps to give the students a broader understanding of the literature. The content of some of these books is mature, and the group discussions allow the students to work together to make sense of the books.

The reason we have not included *Anne Frank: The Diary of a Young Girl* in this particular unit is because in our school district *Anne Frank* is a required part of our eighth-grade English curriculum. We want *all* students to read about her. Because some students are already World War II experts and because other students have no idea that such horrible events ever took place, we feel that *Anne Frank* makes a good starting point for preparing all of the students for the Holocaust stories to come.

Because this Holocaust literature unit will take four weeks to complete, you probably won't want to go into too much depth studying about Anne Frank. Interesting excerpts ought to be enough, although you could give extra credit to students who want to read the entire work. The students may also enjoy reading the screenplay, which takes four or five days. Or you could show the movie, which takes four days. The teacher must take care in choosing the approach of the overall unit, so that students do not become "Holocausted" out by the end. It's easy to overdo this unit because the subject matter is so interesting and so abundant.

We like to schedule this unit for the end of the school year so that it will coincide with our school's social studies unit on World War II. This way, the students can get the historical background from their social studies class to enrich their understanding of the stories in this unit. Conversely, the literature provides the stories of real people that the history books cannot.

This unit could tie in easily with other school subjects, too. Art, music, and science teachers could participate in some way. Maybe even math.

Structure

Each classroom consists of five or six groups of five students, with each group reading a different piece of Holocaust literature. The days in class are divided between reading, group discussions, and a variety of writing assignments.

At the end of the unit, each group will present its book to the class, so that everyone in the class will benefit from all the books.

Here are the books included in this unit:

I Am Fifteen—And I Don't Want to Die! by Christine Arnothy. Scholastic, Inc., 1956. ISBN 0-590-44630-4.

The Cage, by Ruth Minsky Sender. Bantam Books, 1986. ISBN 0-533-27003-6.

Night, by Elie Wiesel. Bantam Books, 1960. ISBN 0-553-27253-5.

The Hiding Place, by Corrie ten Boom. Bantam Books, 1971. ISBN 0-553-25669-6.

The Last Mission, by Harry Mazer. Laurel-Leaf Books, 1979. ISBN 0-440-94797-9.

Mischling, Second Degree, by Ilse Koehn. Puffin Books, 1990. ISBN 0-14-034290-7.

The Upstairs Room, by Johanna Reiss. Harper-Trophy, 1990. ISBN 0-06-440370-X.

In the Mouth of the Wolf, by Rose Zar. Jewish Publication Society, 1983. ISBN 0-8276-0382-7.

Farewell to Manzanar, by Jeanne Wakatsuki Houston and James Houston. Bantam Books, 1973. ISBN 0-553-27258-6.

Kindertransport, by Olga Levy Drucker. Henry Holt and Company, 1992. ISBN 0-8050-1711-9.

Touch Wood, by Renée Roth-Hano. Puffin Books, 1989. ISBN 0-14-034085-8.

Maus I and *Maus II,* by Art Spiegelman. Pantheon Books, 1973–1991. *Maus I* ISBN 0-394-74723-2. *Maus II* ISBN 0-679-72977-1.

To help you decide which of these 12 stories to use, we include a description of each one at the beginning of each individual unit. You can analyze what kinds of students you have and then determine which books would most appeal to them.

How to Use This Unit

How to Begin

Begin by looking over the descriptions of the books to see which ones you would like to use in your class. Choose stories that you feel your students would be most interested in reading. Some of the books may appeal more to boys than to girls or vice versa, but most of the stories will appeal to either gender.

Because the students will be sharing what they learn with the rest of the class at the end of the unit, it's desirable to have the class read a variety of stories: maybe a couple of stories from a Jewish perspective, one from a German, one American, and one Polish, for example. The students should ultimately come away from this experience with an understanding of how people of varied races and creeds were affected by World War II.

Purchasing a book for every student is not necessary. All of the reading can be done in class, which means that if you have several English or reading classes, you can use the same 30 books for all of them. You will need to purchase six copies of each title you choose.

After you have chosen the books you would like to use in this unit, give the students the choice of which books they would like to read. We like to have a "book talk" day. We give a brief summary of each story and pass the books around for the students to look at.

Sometimes students think this unit will be easier if they choose a short book with large print. Explain to the students that all of the lessons are exactly the same length, so the shorter books will have more assignments to go along with them, and the units for the longer books will have more reading and fewer assignments.

At the end of the "book talk" period, we have students write down their top two or three choices, and then we match the students up with the books.

Choosing Groups

In grouping the students, take into consideration what the students want to read, and then decide which students will work well together. The groups should be heterogeneous. Include a couple of top students, a couple of average students, and a lower-end student in each group. Sometimes friends work well together, and sometimes they don't. Sometimes students who don't know each other work well together. Finding out who can't work together might be a good idea as well. We occasionally have a group that simply isn't working out, and in that case, we just plan on working with that group more closely than others. Most groups, however, need little or no guidance from the teacher.

Because of the heterogeneous groups, it really doesn't matter what book each group reads. All of the books will be a little difficult for the low readers, and that's why it's a good idea to have students read the books aloud. Reading aloud also keeps the group at the same place so discussions will be easier.

How to Manage the Papers

The easiest and most effective way of passing out papers, we have found, is to give each student at the very beginning a packet of every reproducible page she or he needs to understand and complete this unit. This way, students can see the day-to-day schedule, as well as the assignments to come. They can even read the guidelines for the class presentation, which is included in the Appendix. There should be no surprises. The exception would be the Answer Sheets that are included in the Appendix. These should not be distributed until after each assignment is completed.

Students should turn in assignments as soon as they complete them. There are two different ways to manage the completed assignments. You can give each group a folder to keep completed assignments in, and then at the end of each day or week, collect the folders and grade them. The advantage of this method is that all the assignments for each group are together—they're not mixed in with other groups. Or you can simply have all students in a class put their assignments in a single basket. The advantage of this method is that the teacher doesn't have to collect folders, and all the papers for a single class are together.

The sooner papers are returned to the students, and the sooner students begin to understand how everything will be graded, the more seriously they will take each assignment. Included in each student's packet should be a grade sheet for the book that he or she is reading. As the students finish the assignments and turn them in, they should check them off on the grade sheet where it says "Student ✓." After the assignments are returned, the students can enter the number of points they received for the assignments and how many points they were worth, if that information isn't already on the grade sheet. It might also be a good idea to have a grading scale on the grade sheet, too, so students can estimate how many points they'll need to get a certain grade.

Time Management

Probably the biggest worry for both the teachers and the students is trying to keep up with this unit's day-to-day schedule. Please regard this schedule as simply a guideline. Since most students read at different levels, you will find that not all group members will complete the daily assignments at the same time. Students typically fix this problem themselves by reading aloud, taking assignments home, or by checking books out. One advantage of using heterogeneous groups is that

the books can be read aloud, eliminating the problem of varying reading levels.

If the teacher finds that most of the groups in a class are behind, a "catch-up" day can be incorporated. Our guidelines for what should be accomplished during a day are designed to keep the students moving—they have lots to do every day. If you find that your students are falling behind in the day structure, let them know that the activities of a certain day should follow the activities of the day before. There's a progression.

If a student is absent, the group can brief that student on what they read when he or she was absent. They can also help that student with the assignment that may have been due. This is another advantage of having groups. If a student is absent for an extended time, send a book home, and he or she can work on it alone. The student will already have the assignments and know exactly what to do. You will just need to let the student know how far to go.

Grading

First of all, you will need to decide how many points you want this entire Holocaust unit to be worth. If you look at the grade sheets, you will notice that the Points Possible column has been left blank for the teacher's discretion. Figure out how many points you want each assignment to be worth. For the books that have more assignments, a certain assignment might be worth less than a similar assignment for another book that has fewer assignments. Also keep in mind the difficulty of an assignment when assigning points. A long and involved assignment should be worth more than a "fill-in-the-blanks" one.

The fastest and easiest way to grade all the papers that come in is to give them a +, a ✓, or a –. If an assignment is worth 10 points, then make a + worth 10 points, a ✓ worth 7 or 8 points, and a – worth 5 or 6 points. The teacher may also keep a grade sheet for each student in a notebook. Then, as assignments are turned in, the teacher can fill in the points. At the end of the unit, the teacher can give a copy of the grade sheet to each student, and the student can compare it with his or her own record.

For group discussions, we evaluate the record of what was discussed, and all group members will receive the same grade from the paper that the Secretary turned in. Most assignments, however, are graded individually. Please emphasize that all the students in a group will *not* receive the same grade for the unit. It is possible for one group member to get an A, and another group member to fail.

Each student will also receive a grade for group participation. Throughout the course of the unit, the teacher should be observing group members to see how they are participating. Most groups will let the teacher know which students are not pulling their weight. At the completion of the unit, the students will complete a group evaluation form. This should be completed in an organized, efficient manner to take up the least amount of time. Each group member will receive a sheet of paper with five spaces. They need to put each of their group members' names in the spaces provided, including their own, in the same order. They will give a score to each person, and all the teacher has to do is put the papers together, staple, and then cut them apart. Then you should have all the evaluations of a single student stapled together.

Essays

For writing assignments, we have included a reproducible essay form in the Appendix. At first, it might seem to be a waste of paper to provide a form for student writing. But we have found that the students take the essays more seriously when they see the form—it seems to trigger a sense of formality for the assignment. Before we started using an official essay form, we found that students sometimes didn't take the essay assignment seriously, and they might write only a paragraph (if that!). To make this form even more effective, we have already given students essay-writing experience throughout the year on similar forms. When our students see the essay form,

they know that the essay will need to be several paragraphs long, cohesive, well-organized, in pen, spelled right, and probably a final draft.

Group Presentations

At the end of the reading, the students will be preparing a group presentation. This is actually the most important and fun part of the unit. Let your students know from the beginning that they will be doing a presentation to the class, because this knowledge makes the students more serious about their reading and their studying. The guidelines for the class presentation are given at the end of each unit, and they're all the same.

In the Appendix you will find a form for evaluating group presentations. Have each group turn in a paper that explains what each member has done for preparing and presenting the story to the class. The presentation grade should be an individual grade based on individual effort rather than a group grade.

If a student is absent on the day of the presentation, the group can present on another day, or the absent person might give a presentation to the teacher at an appointed time.

Quizzes

Following their presentation, each group needs to give the rest of the class a five-point quiz. You can decide what form the quiz should take, or you can let the students decide how they'll set up their quiz. The group is then responsible for grading the quizzes and getting them back to the other students. We have included a quiz-taking form in the Appendix to help you keep track of all the quiz grades.

Use your own discretion in handling the situation when students are absent for a quiz. Most teachers already have an absence policy in place.

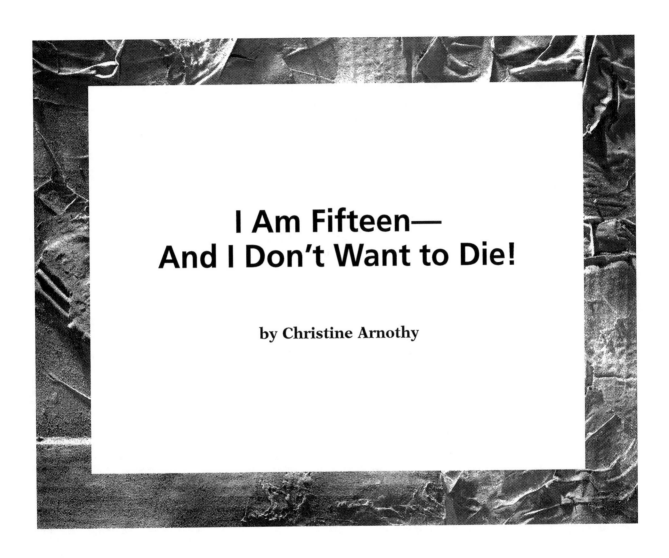

I Am Fifteen—
And I Don't Want to Die!

by Christine Arnothy

Name _____ Date _____

I Am Fifteen—And I Don't Want to Die!
by Christine Arnothy

To the Student

When you think about World War II, you probably think of Germans and Jews. Actually, the war affected people in all parts of the world, which is why it was called a world war. The story you are about to read took place in Hungary, and the author is *not* Jewish. Life was not hellish just for the Jews, but for everyone who lived in Europe at the time of the war. Christine Arnothy was simply a Hungarian girl whose family got caught in the middle of the fighting. And she, like thousands of other Europeans, endured unbelievable conditions to survive the nightmare.

When you read this story, think about how *you* would have reacted to these events. Would you have had the courage and strength to live in a cellar for months? How long could you go with very little food? How long could you do without electricity?

Notice the *attitudes* of the people in hiding as you read. Did they harbor hatred toward the Germans? Did they have revenge in mind? What about their attitudes toward each other? When civilization as they knew it in Hungary broke down and the people were reduced to living like animals, how did they behave?

When it comes time to do your book presentation to the class, be sure to emphasize that Christine Arnothy was not Jewish. Also emphasize where the story takes place. If possible, show Hungary on a map so the whole class can see this other country that Germany occupied. Be sure to explain to the other students what the living conditions were like. How was it that people survived? Was it because of their attitudes or because of something that they did?

Name _____   Date _____

Unit Outline:

I Am Fifteen—And I Don't Want to Die!

by Christine Arnothy

Day 1:
1. Assign a role to each group member:
   (a) *Secretary:* Someone to record the group assignments and discussions. In recording the discussions, the Secretary should describe the general discussion—who thought what—and then describe how the discussion ended. Was there a consensus?
   (b) *Taskmaster:* Someone to read instructions each day and keep the group on task.
   (c) *Assignment Collector:* Someone to make sure all assignments get turned in each day.
   (d) *Librarian:* Someone to get the books and return them each day. The Librarian will also complete any research required.
   (e) *Activity Director:* Someone to organize group activities.
2. Identify group members who would like to read aloud.
3. Complete the Questionnaire sheet on your own. Upon completion, discuss your responses with your group. Why did you choose the items you did? Does your group have the same or differing opinions? Justify or defend your responses on the back of your paper.*
4. The Librarian needs to get the books at this point.
5. The Taskmaster will read the introductory material aloud to the group so that all group members will have a good idea of what will be expected during the unit.
6. If there's still time left in the class period, begin reading aloud.

Day 2:
1. Read Chapter 1.
2. Fill out Day 2 Section Summary/Title sheet. This can be a group effort; however, each group member will be responsible for his/her own paper. This assignment will be turned in when you're finished reading the book.
3. There are so many people staying in the cellar, it's hard to keep track of them. This assignment will help. Make a chart of all the characters. Include the following information:
   (a) name
   (b) physical description (height, weight, hair color, eye color, etc.)
   (c) profession, hobbies, interests

   Do this assignment on your own paper, and it will be due at the end of the period today.

Day 3:
1. Read Chapter 2.
2. Fill out Section Summary/Title sheet for these pages.
3. Do Semicolon worksheet. When everyone in the group is finished, ask the teacher for the answer sheet so you can correct your work.

---

* All group discussions must be written up by the Secretary and turned in at the completion of the discussion.

Unit Outline: *I Am Fifteen—And I Don't Want to Die!*

Day 4:
1. Read Chapter 3.
2. Fill out Section Summary/Title sheet.
3. Group discussion: Identify a turning point for the author on p. 20. Explain why this event is a turning point.*
4. Group activity: Scan through the first three chapters and make a list of all the references to Pista. How do the others see him? In the first line of the book, for example: 1. "deliverer" (p. 1)*

Day 5:
1. Read Chapters 4 and 5.
2. Fill out Section Summary/Title sheet.
3. Tense activity. Look at the beginning of chapter 4 on p. 30. Notice that this book is written in the past tense. If Arnothy had wanted, she could have written this book in the present tense to show that she is still reliving this situation. Present tense makes the story seem like a snapshot—never changing with time. Rewrite the first four paragraphs of this chapter in the present tense on your own paper. Then reread the passage to yourself before turning it in, so you can see how the change in tense can change the feeling of the story. This is how you start:

   > For two days we have not had a drop of water. Ilus uses the last half-glassful to make some warm gruel for the baby with the remainder of the dried milk . . .

   Turn in your assignment when finished.

Day 6:
1. Read Chapters 6 and 7.
2. Fill out Section Summary/Title sheet.
3. Group discussion: What is it that Pista does for the group? Could they have survived without him? Was he *really* special? What do you think he looked like? Have the Secretary record the outcome of this discussion to turn in. Was there a consensus, or was the group divided in thought? Who thought what? Due today.

Day 7:
1. Read Chapters 8 and 9.
2. Fill out Section Summary/Title sheet.
3. Group discussion: What is the change that occurs on p. 67? What does this change tell you about human nature?*
4. Do Copy Change assignment. Read the directions carefully. Because this assignment may take a little longer to complete, you may have to finish at home. Be sure to rewrite your finished product on notebook paper in paragraph form.

Day 8:
1. Read Chapters 10 and 11.
2. Fill out Section Summary/Title sheet.
3. Do Figurative Language worksheet. When you're finished, ask the teacher for the answer sheet so you can correct your work. Turn in your assignment.

---

* All group discussions must be written up by the Secretary and turned in at the completion of the discussion.

4   *Holocaust Literature: Study Guides to 12 Stories of Courage*

Unit Outline: *I Am Fifteen—And I Don't Want to Die!*

Day 9:
1. Read Chapter 12.
2. Fill out Section Summary/Title sheet.
3. Do Colon worksheet. When you're finished, ask the teacher for the answer sheet so you can correct your work. Then answer the question at the bottom of the worksheet and turn in your assignment.

Day 10:
1. Read Chapter 13.
2. Do the final Section Summary/Title sheet and turn in your assignment.
3. Group discussion:
   (a) Does the picture on the cover go with the book? Why or why not?
   (b) What role does religion play in this story?*

Day 11:
1. Do the Cause and Effect flowchart. The teacher will provide instructions.
2. Have each member of the group choose a different character in the story and make a flowchart or a time line or a list that shows what happens to him or her throughout the story. Use plain white paper and colored pencils or markers.

   (In preparation for tomorrow's assignment, have the Librarian go to the library and find a short biography of Christine Arnothy to bring to class. *Something About the Author,* or another bibliographical reference, is a good source for this information.)

Day 12:
1. Discuss the Importance Chart as a group, and have the Secretary record the group consensus to turn in.*
2. Read the information about Christine Arnothy that you found in the library.
3. Group discussion: Based on the information about the author and from what you've learned about her in the book, what kind of a character description could you write about her? Discuss this as a group, and then have the Librarian record the group's ideas to turn in.*

Day 13:
Begin working on Holocaust Literature handout. The teacher will provide instructions. Use the Holocaust Essay Form for your final copy of the written assignment.

Days 14–17:
Begin planning the presentation that your group will give to the class. The Taskmaster will read the instructions from the Class Presentation sheet. The group should formulate some ideas with the Secretary taking notes. During the next four days, your group should be putting together your presentation and related assignments, as well as rehearsing for the class presentation.

Determine who will be responsible for what parts. Before you present, you will need to turn in a paper neatly written in ink with all of your names in the heading that will outline the responsibilities for each group member. Each member will be graded individually for his/her part in the presentation.*

Days 18–20:
Class presentations. There will be a five-question quiz at the end of each presentation.

---

* All group discussions must be written up by the Secretary and turned in at the completion of the discussion.

I Am Fifteen—And I Don't Want to Die!

by Christine Arnothy
Day 1: Questionnaire

Read the following questions and determine for yourself the answers you think are best. You may choose two or three items per question.

1. *What words best describe* **prejudice**?

_____ obstinate	_____ single-minded	_____ biased
_____ forceful	_____ conceited	_____ ignorant
_____ stubborn	_____ poor	_____ wealthy
_____ judgmental	_____ unloved	_____ opinionated

2. *What do you think causes a person to become prejudiced?*

_____ He/She was just born that way.

_____ His/Her parents taught him/her to be that way by their example.

_____ He/She observes incidents on television and at school.

_____ He/She lives in an area where he/she is in the minority.

_____ He/She lives in an area where he/she is in the vast majority.

_____ He/She has been the victim in a race-related incident.

_____ He/She has been the victim in an ethnic-related incident.

_____ His/Her religion teaches supremacy of one race over another.

3. *How would you recognize a prejudiced person?*

_____ From the way he/she lives.

_____ From his/her facial expressions.

_____ From his/her actions toward athletes, comedians, or politicians of different ethnic, racial, or religious backgrounds.

_____ From the way he/she teases, taunts people.

4. *How would you cure a prejudiced person?*

_____ With love and kindness, understanding.

_____ With reasoning and knowledge.

_____ By giving him/her a taste of his/her own medicine.

_____ By getting someone to beat or frighten him/her.

_____ There is no cure.

Name _____   Date _____

I Am Fifteen—And I Don't Want to Die!
Summaries and Titles

Directions:

1. Each member of the group will keep track of each of the section summaries in the book and turn in this assignment at the end of the reading. **Each of you will also be responsible for predicting future events based on what you have just read.**

2. After reading each day, look back over the pages read and think about what you might title the reading for that day if you were the author of the book. After the group members have individually decided on chapter titles, have a group discussion on why the titles were given. Which title does the group agree is the most accurate?

	Section Summary and Prediction	Section Title
Day 2 Pages read:		Why?
Day 3 Pages read:		Why?
Day 4 Pages read:		Why?
Day 5 Pages read:		Why?

(continued)

Holocaust Literature:
Study Guides to 12 Stories of Courage

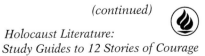

I Am Fifteen—And I Don't Want to Die!
Summaries and Titles (continued)

	Section Summary and Prediction	Section Title
Day 6 Pages read:		Why?
Day 7 Pages read:		Why?
Day 8 Pages read:		Why?
Day 9 Pages read:		Why?
Day 10 Pages read:		Why?

I Am Fifteen—And I Don't Want to Die!
Day 3: Semicolons

A semicolon is a punctuation mark used between sentences that are close to each other in meaning. The period part of this punctuation shows that the writer knows that there are two sentences; the comma part lessens the separation.

The following sentences were taken from this novel, but the semicolons have been replaced by commas. Insert the semicolons where you think they belong. Then ask the teacher for the answer sheet so you can check your work by looking up the original sentences in the book.

1. Unbelieving, we stared at the speaker, then, on a common impulse, we decided to verify his words with our own eyes.

2. The powerful river that used to carry pretty pleasure boats seemed to be bruised by contact with the twisted ironwork, it seethed into giddy whirlpools and, in its impotent rage, hurled great blocks of ice against the quays on either bank.

3. An inexpressible feeling drove us together, it was frightening to be alone.

4. The flow increased, we saw, with horror, a very thin but ever-increasing stream of water spreading over the floor.

5. Two months of the siege of Budapest had left their mark on my father, his shoulders were bowed and he had let his beard grow, making his appearance rather pitiful, which was just as well in those days.

6. Here, two days before, they had attempted a breakthrough and were all mown down, the streetcar tracks were running with their blood.

7. There was less destruction in the next district we went through, the Russians had occupied these residential streets quickly.

Holocaust Literature:
Study Guides to 12 Stories of Courage

I Am Fifteen—And I Don't Want to Die!
Day 7: Copy Change Assignment

This paragraph is found on p. 60:

In this strange, smoky atmosphere things no longer had any reality: the courtyard, the street, the whole city, blurred in a ghastly light, looked like a landscape on the moon. Abandoned weapons lay everywhere. Opposite us, a house had collapsed on its inmates whom death had surprised in the middle of their horrible fight against suffocation. There, on the right, was the fragment of a fourth floor apartment where a piano hung supported only by a few bricks; of the room next door, which must have been a bathroom, nothing remained but a wall with a towel rack.

Assignment:

In your mind, picture a disaster that you remember. For me it was when I was in second grade, and my dad, after watching a commercial on TV about a soap product that kids could use to sculpt things, decided to create his own product. Basically, what he did was to take a whole box of laundry detergent and mix it with enough water to make a paste, and then let my two sisters and me have a fun afternoon "sculpting" the soap paste into whatever we wanted. It was, however, a huge mess, and we were still finding soap globs on furniture for years afterward.

In this sticky, gooey kitchen things no longer could be considered really clean: the kitchen table, the floor, the whole room, glued together with a white paste, looked like that day after a snowstorm. Soap globs stuck everywhere. On the kitchen table, a castle with sagging walls threatened Barbie and Ken, unaware, enjoying their first date. There, in the middle of the room, was the hand mixer stuck forever on low; its little engine sounded like a low battery in the middle of winter.

You can use this generating frame below to help you with the wording:

In this _____ , _____ (place) things no longer _____ : the _____ , the _____ , the whole _____ , _____ ed _____ , looked like _____ . _____ (verb) _____ every-where. _____ (Place) _____ , a/an _____ (verb) _____ _____ _____ . There on the/in the _____ (direction) _____ , was _____ ; _____ (a related idea goes here after the semicolon) _____ .

If you need help with this assignment, refer to the paragraph from the book and to the paragraph above to see what kind of information goes in each blank. You really have quite a bit of freedom to change the words in order to describe the scene as you remember it. Good luck!

© 1997 J. Weston Walch, Publisher

Holocaust Literature:
Study Guides to 12 Stories of Courage

I Am Fifteen—And I Don't Want to Die!
Day 8: Figurative Language

Christine Arnothy's writing throughout this book is vivid with imagery. She makes ample use of literary devices. Read the definitions of these kinds of devices and then label each quotation below with the correct term. When you're finished, ask the teacher for the answer sheet and check your work by looking on the page numbers given.

Simile: A comparison between unlike things using the words *like* or *as*.
Example: Tears flowed like wine.

Irony: Expression in which the intended meaning of the words is the opposite of their usual sense; or an event or result that is the opposite of what is expected.

Personification: Treating an inanimate object as if it had human qualities.
Example: The wind challenged the team to excel.

_____ 1. The Russian bullets had shipped right into his bedroom, completely disregarding his wife's Swiss nationality! (p. 6)

_____ 2. The town was burning all around us while we shivered on our heap of coal. (p. 3)

_____ 3. In my eyes, Pista had become a dazzling hero. He was like the Count of Monte Cristo. (p. 15)

_____ 4. "An ammunition train blows up just beside us, the restaurant is packed with high explosives; the steel of the cannons is melting, they're firing so much to use up the shells before the Russians arrive, and these wretched animals will perish of hunger and thirst!" (pp. 23–24)

_____ 5. Like an apocalyptic flood, sweeping all before it, fresh waves of soldiers invaded the houses. (p. 68)

_____ 6. The sun began to shine. Its sad rays groped feebly among the ruins of the dead town; the watery March light showed the city to be a more ghastly sight than ever. (p. 66)

_____ 7. The destruction of the bridges had eclipsed all other fears . . . yet this indifference itself was perhaps the most frightening thing of all. (p. 28)

_____ 8. Had he, in his final agony, tried to send a last message to his family by staring at their pictures? It was as if, at the Budagyongye stop, he were waiting for the coming of some celestial, redeeming streetcar. (p. 76)

Holocaust Literature:
Study Guides to 12 Stories of Courage

I Am Fifteen—And I Don't Want to Die!
Day 9: Colons

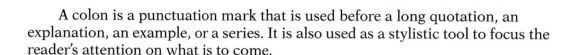

A colon is a punctuation mark that is used before a long quotation, an explanation, an example, or a series. It is also used as a stylistic tool to focus the reader's attention on what is to come.

The following sentences were taken from this novel, but the colons have been removed. Insert the colon where you think it belongs. When you're done, ask the teacher for the answers so you can check your work by looking up the original sentences in the book.

1. Waking up was always torture reality, the horrible cellar, the smelly candle and the hollow-eyed shapes wandering about in the half-light.

2. The days dragged by fearful nightmares and battles against a world of phantoms.

3. A sudden shock ran through me as if I had touched a live wire, reviving all my memories at once our life in the cellar, the marriage of Eve and Gabriel, the death of brave Pista.

4. But remember this, Justice and charity come before everything.

5. She and I planned to meet again in two days, I took a long time deciding the exact hour for she proposed five o'clock and I, a quarter past.

6. He seemed to be smiling in a way that meant, "I'm the first one ready. Now we can go!"

7. The guide never stopped grumbling, "This is the last time I do this job with old people . . ."

8. This was where I was at home, here where spirits met again in the luminous void that stretched between the two halves of the world.

Why would the author choose to use colons in these sentences rather than commas?

Holocaust Literature:

Study Guides to 12 Stories of Courage

I Am Fifteen—And I Don't Want to Die!
Day 11: Cause and Effect

Show how the events in a novel determine future events by filling in the squares with causes and effects from *I Am Fifteen—And I Don't Want to Die!* Begin each sentence with *Since* or *Because*. When you begin a sentence with either of these two words, you create a complex sentence, and there needs to be a comma at the end of the first clause. The first one has been done for you.

Because the Germans have occupied Budapest, Christine and her family are forced to live in their cellar for safety reasons.

Since they're living in the cellar,

Holocaust Literature:
Study Guides to 12 Stories of Courage

I Am Fifteen—And I Don't Want to Die!
Day 12: Importance Chart

On the lines below, list the 10 events (in order of occurrence) that your group considers the most important events in the book. Then explain why.

1. _____ ,

   because _____ .

2. _____ ,

   because _____ .

3. _____ ,

   because _____ .

4. _____ ,

   because _____ .

5. _____ ,

   because _____ .

6. _____ ,

   because _____ .

7. _____ ,

   because _____ .

8. _____ ,

   because _____ .

9. _____ ,

   because _____ .

10. _____ ,

   because _____ .

Name _____ Date _____

I Am Fifteen—And I Don't Want to Die!
Grading Sheet

Assignment	Possible Points	Student ✓	Teacher ✓	Points
1. Questionnaire Responses				
2. Chart of Characters				
3. Day 3: Semicolons				
4. Day 4: Group Discussion				
5. Day 4: Group Activity				
6. Day 5: Tense Activity				
7. Day 6: Group Discussion				
8. Day 7: Group Discussion				
9. Day 7: Copy Change				
10. Day 8: Figurative Language				
11. Day 9: Colons				
12. Day 10: Group Discussion				
13. Summaries and Titles				
14. Day 11: Cause and Effect				
15. Day 11: Character Assignment				
16. Day 12: Importance Chart				
17. Day 12: Group Discussion				
18. Day 13: Holocaust Literature				
19. Holocaust Essay				
20. Character Bag				
21. Class Presentation				
22. Class Quizzes				
23. Group Participation				
			Total Pts.	
			Grade	

Holocaust Literature:
Study Guides to 12 Stories of Courage

The Cage

by Ruth Minsky Sender

The Cage
by Ruth Minsky Sender

To the Student

The story you are about to read is a true story that takes place in Poland. The author was 16 years old in 1939 when the events began. During the next five years, at a time when most girls are still figuring out who they are and what they want to be when they grow up, Riva Minsky became the only parent of her brothers. While this in itself would be a huge burden to a teenage girl, Riva also found herself in the middle of the German occupation of Poland. She and her family were then forced to live in the ghetto—a confined area which Jews were not allowed to leave.

This story is divided into two parts. The first part takes place in the ghetto, and the second part takes place in the concentration camps. You have probably already heard terrible stories about conditions in the concentration camps, so take note of Riva's belief that life in the ghetto was about all that she could possibly endure. She and the other Jews had no idea that their life would get even worse. Where do you think she got the courage and the strength to survive? Why do you think she even *wanted* to survive?

Notice the *attitudes* of the Jewish people as you read. Did they harbor hatred toward the Germans? Did they have revenge in mind? What about their attitudes toward each other? When civilization as they knew it in Poland broke down, and the inhabitants of the concentration camps were reduced to living like animals, how did they behave?

When it comes time to do your book presentation to the class, emphasize where this story takes place. If possible, show Poland on a map to illustrate where it's located in relation to Germany. Probably the most remarkable part of this book is Riva Minsky's strong will to survive in even the most unimaginable circumstances. How will you convey this idea to the class?

Unit Outline:

The Cage

by Ruth Minsky Sender

Day 1:

1. Assign a role to each group member:

   (a) *Secretary:* Someone to record the group assignments and discussions. In recording the discussions, the Secretary should describe the general discussion—who thought what—and then describe how the discussion ended. Was there a consensus?

   (b) *Taskmaster:* Someone to read instructions each day and keep the group on task.

   (c) *Assignment Collector:* Someone to make sure all assignments get turned in each day.

   (d) *Librarian:* Someone to get the books and return them each day. The Librarian will also complete any research required.

   (e) *Activity Director:* Someone to organize group activities.

2. Identify group members who would like to read aloud.

3. Complete the Questionnaire sheet on your own. Upon completion, discuss your responses with your group. Why did you choose the items you did? Does your group have the same or differing opinions? Justify or defend your responses on the back of your paper.*

4. The Librarian needs to get the books at this point.

5. The Taskmaster will read the introductory material aloud to the group so that all group members will have a good idea of what will be expected during the unit.

6. If there's still time left in the class period, begin reading aloud.

Day 2:

1. Read Chapters 1–4 aloud.

2. Fill out Day 2 Section Summary/Title sheet. This can be a group effort; however, each group member will be responsible for turning in his/her own paper. Turn in this assignment when you have finished reading the book.

3. This book has a lot of characters, and a character chart will help you keep track of who is who. Begin making a chart of all the characters on your own paper. Each student will turn in a final, polished chart at the end of the unit; so you should work on a rough draft during the reading and rewrite your chart when you have completed the novel. Make sure you include all of the more important characters. Include the following information:

   (a) name (you may include their relationship to the main character)
   (b) physical description (height, weight, hair color, eye color, etc.)
   (c) profession, hobbies, interests

Day 3:

1. Read Chapters 5–9 aloud.

2. Fill out Section Summary/Title sheet.

---

* All group discussions must be written up by the Secretary and turned in at the completion of the discussion.

Unit Outline: *The Cage*

3. Group discussion: You have probably noticed by now that the book is written in the present tense. Both the beginning of the book and the flashback (the main plot) are written in the present tense. Why do you think Sender chose this tense? Brainstorm some possible reasons that your group can think of, and turn the answers in today.*

Day 4:
1. Read Chapters 10–14.
2. Fill out Section Summary/Title sheet.
3. Verb tense assignment. Take a look at the last two paragraphs in Chapter 13 and the first two paragraphs in Chapter 14. Notice that Sender wrote this book in the present tense. Using your own paper, rewrite the four paragraphs in the past tense to see the difference in the effect. For example, the first sentence will go like this: "My eyes **were** full of tears." Group members can help each other, but each student will turn in a separate paper. Finish tomorrow in class if there wasn't enough time today. Turn in when finished.

Day 5:
1. Read Chapters 15–19.
2. Fill out Section Summary/Title sheet.
3. Finish verb tense assignment, if necessary.

Day 6:
1. Read Chapters 19–22.
2. Fill out Section Summary/Title sheet.
3. Homework assignment: Snapshot. See handout.

Day 7:
1. Read Chapters 23–25.
2. Fill out Section Summary/Title sheet.
3. Work on Snapshot story, if needed.
4. Group discussion: Sender comments frequently on the sunshine or springtime or flowers as she tells her story, and she does this throughout the book. Why does she do this? Discuss this as a group and submit one paper with the group's ideas.*

Day 8:
1. Read Chapters 26–31.
2. Fill out Section Summary/Title sheet.

Day 9:
1. Read Chapters 32–36.
2. Fill out Section Summary/Title sheet.
3. Look up "cage" in the dictionary. Then, as a group, begin making a list of the cages in this book. Some of the cages are physical—like the ghetto, for example. Others are more abstract—like one's race, for example. Begin this list today, and add to it every day when you're working on your summary sheets. Then, when you're finished reading the book, turn in one copy of the list for your group.*

Day 10:
1. Read Chapters 37–40.
2. Fill out Section Summary/Title sheet.

---

* All group discussions must be written up by the Secretary and turned in at the completion of the discussion.

20 *Holocaust Literature: Study Guides to 12 Stories of Courage*

Unit Outline: *The Cage*

3. Group discussion: Prioritize the following things in the order of importance you think they play in the author's life toward the end of the book.

shelter	food	religion
family	books/learning	morality
life	friends	happiness

After you have listed these in order of importance, tell why you put them in the order you did. Work on this as a group.*

Day 11: 1. The teacher will give the directions for the Cause and Effect flowchart. Wait until after the reading to do this assignment.

2. Read Chapters 41–43.

3. Fill out Section Summary/Title sheet.

Day 12: 1. Read Chapters 44 to the end.

2. Section Summary/Title sheet due today from each group member.

3. Group discussion of the Importance Chart. Turn one in for the group.*

Day 13: 1. Begin working on Holocaust Literature handout. The teacher will provide instructions. Use the Holocaust Essay Form for your final copy of the written assignment.

Days 14–17: 1. Writing assignment due.

2. Begin planning the presentation that your group will give to the class. The Taskmaster will read the instructions from the project presentation sheet. The group should formulate some ideas, with the Secretary taking notes. During the next four days, your group should be putting together your presentation and related assignments, as well as rehearsing for the class presentation.

Determine who will be responsible for what parts. Before you present, you will need to turn in a paper neatly written in ink with all of your names in the heading that will outline the responsibilities for each group member. Each member will be graded individually for his/her part in the presentation.*

Days 18–20: Class presentations. There will be a five-question quiz at the end of each presentation.

Questions:

Provide time to answer questions from the class.

_____

* All group discussions must be written up by the Secretary and turned in at the completion of the discussion.

Name _____   Date _____

The Cage
by Ruth Minsky Sender
Day 1: Questionnaire

Read the following questions and determine for yourself the answers you think are best. You may choose two or three items per question.

1. *What words best describe* **prejudice**?

   _____ obstinate   _____ single-minded   _____ biased

   _____ forceful   _____ conceited   _____ ignorant

   _____ stubborn   _____ poor   _____ wealthy

   _____ judgmental   _____ unloved   _____ opinionated

2. *What do you think causes a person to become prejudiced?*

   _____ He/She was just born that way.

   _____ His/Her parents taught him/her to be that way by their example.

   _____ He/She observes incidents on television and at school.

   _____ He/She lives in an area where he/she is in the minority.

   _____ He/She lives in an area where he/she is in the vast majority.

   _____ He/She has been the victim in a race-related incident.

   _____ He/She has been the victim in an ethnic-related incident.

   _____ His/Her religion teaches supremacy of one race over another.

3. *How would you recognize a prejudiced person?*

   _____ From the way he/she lives.

   _____ From his/her facial expressions.

   _____ From his/her actions toward athletes, comedians, or politicians of different ethnic, racial, or religious backgrounds.

   _____ From the way he/she teases, taunts people.

4. *How would you cure a prejudiced person?*

   _____ With love and kindness, understanding.

   _____ With reasoning and knowledge.

   _____ By giving him/her a taste of his/her own medicine.

   _____ By getting someone to beat or frighten him/her.

   _____ There is no cure.

Holocaust Literature:
Study Guides to 12 Stories of Courage

Name _____ Date _____

The Cage
Summaries and Titles

Directions:

1. Each member of the group will keep track of each of the section summaries in the book and turn in this assignment at the end of the reading. **Each of you will also be responsible for predicting future events based on what you have just read.**

2. After reading each day, look back over the pages read and think about what you might title the reading for that day if you were the author of the book. After the group members have individually decided on chapter titles, have a group discussion on why the titles were given. Which title does the group agree is the most accurate?

	Section Summary and Prediction	Section Title
Day 2 Pages read:		Why?
Day 3 Pages read:		Why?
Day 4 Pages read:		Why?
Day 5 Pages read:		Why?

(continued)

Holocaust Literature:
Study Guides to 12 Stories of Courage

The Cage
Summaries and Titles *(continued)*

	Section Summary and Prediction	Section Title
Day 6 Pages read:		Why?
Day 7 Pages read:		Why?
Day 8 Pages read:		Why?
Day 9 Pages read:		Why?
Day 10 Pages read:		Why?

(continued)

The Cage
Summaries and Titles *(continued)*

	Section Summary and Prediction	**Section Title**
Day 11 Pages read:		Why?
Day 12 Pages read:		Why?

Holocaust Literature:
Study Guides to 12 Stories of Courage

The Cage
Day 6: Snapshot Assignment

Think of a photograph you have—either a picture in your memory or in an actual snapshot in a photo album. Probably the picture will be of an event that really stands out in your mind because of some strong emotion attached to it. Tell the story descriptively and with dialogue about that snapshot/memory in the **present tense**. You'll notice that the present tense makes the memory seem as if it's standing still—as in a snapshot.

Here's an example of an experience that is not based on a real photograph, yet you can tell it left an indelible image in the author's mind:

After taking a long look at the summit of the bunny hill, three-year-old Brad quickly decides not to take up skiing. His protests don't faze me, however.

"This is going to be so much fun, Brad!"

Situating his stiff, reluctant body between my knees, I grab hold of the rope tow. But the strength in my hands is too inadequate to pull us anywhere. The rope zips though my fingers, shredding my gloves. Then, with more determination this time, I manage to grip the rope tightly enough to carry both Brad and me upward.

"Aha!" I think. "Wait till Brad sees how much fun this will be!"

Just as I am congratulating myself on how well I have handled the boy, I realize that something is terribly wrong. Brad is no longer gripped between my legs, but instead is sitting on my skis! I have no choice but to let go of the rope tow to put Brad back on his feet again. If only life were so simple.

Having stayed up until midnight the night before, this three-year-old is in no mood to humor his mother, and decides instead to let loose his emotions. His loud wails are heard by everyone at Bogus Basin, and a very long line of skiers has meanwhile formed at the bottom of the bunny hill, patiently waiting for us to clear the rope tow track so they can have a turn.

By this time, Brad and I are hopelessly tangled and slowly sliding downhill. Furiously I try to stand up, but my skis are behind me . . . and crossed. The growing line at the bottom of the hill eats at me as I furiously try to free Brad and me from the enemy tow track. Nothing helps.

Stopping a moment to look around for help, I notice the crowd staring at us with curious fascination. Now I know what zoo animals feel like.

Finally, someone in the audience yells some advice: "Take off your skis!"

Of course. Why haven't I thought of it myself? With a single, simple movement, I yank both of my skis off and Brad's as well. Adrenalin allows me to carry four skis in one arm and Brad in the other as I storm down the bunny hill on foot. It's nap time. Brad's fun is over.

Name _____   Date _____

The Cage
Day 11: Cause and Effect

Show how the events in a novel determine future events by filling in the squares with causes and effects from *The Cage*. Begin each sentence with *Since* or *Because*. When you begin a sentence with either of these two words, you create a complex sentence, and there needs to be a comma at the end of the first clause. The first one has been done for you.

Because the Germans have taken over Lodz, Poland, 16 year-old Riva Minsky and her family are forced to live in a ghetto—a closed-in neighborhood.

Since they're living in the ghetto,

Holocaust Literature:
Study Guides to 12 Stories of Courage

The Cage
Day 12: Importance Chart

On the lines below, list the 10 events (in order of occurrence) that your group considers the most important events in the book. Then explain why.

1. _____ ,

   because _____ .

2. _____ ,

   because _____ .

3. _____ ,

   because _____ .

4. _____ ,

   because _____ .

5. _____ ,

   because _____ .

6. _____ ,

   because _____ .

7. _____ ,

   because _____ .

8. _____ ,

   because _____ .

9. _____ ,

   because _____ .

10. _____ ,

   because _____ .

Name _____   Date _____

The Cage
Grading Sheet

Assignment	Possible Points	Student ✓	Teacher ✓	Points
1. Questionnaire Responses				
2. Section Summaries/Titles				
3. Chart of Characters				
4. Day 3: Group Discussion				
5. Day 4: Verb Tense Assignment				
6. Day 6: Snapshot				
7. Day 7: Group Discussion				
8. Day 9: List of Cages				
9. Day 10: Group Discussion				
10. Day 11: Cause and Effect				
11. Day 12: Importance Chart				
12. Day 13: Holocaust Literature				
13. Holocaust Essay				
14. Character Bag				
15. Class Presentation				
16. Class Quizzes				
17. Group Participation				
			Total Pts.	
			Grade	

Night

by Elie Wiesel

Name _____ Date _____

Night

by Elie Wiesel

To the Student

The story you are about to read is an autobiographical account of the author's experiences as a Jew during World War II. When he chose to put those experiences into book form, most publishing companies did not want to publish his account because it was "too depressing." Elie Wiesel persisted and with good cause. He knew that the world had to hear his story, no matter how gruesome or depressing, so that everyone would know what really happened.

Night takes place in many different countries, but it begins with Elie as a young boy in Sighet, Transylvania. Because they were Jewish, his family was forced to move to a ghetto and from there to the concentration camps of Birkenau, Auschwitz, Buna, and Buchenwald.

Elie had wanted to study the cabbala (the beliefs and customs behind the Jewish religion) in the hopes of becoming a religious leader in his community. As the war progressed and Elie was forced to witness the horrors of persecution and man's inhumanity to man, he began to wonder if there was a God.

As you are reading, notice the reactions and attitudes of the prisoners. How do the prisoners survive? To what lengths would they go in order to live one more day? Could you do the same? When conditions broke down and the prisoners were treated as animals, how did they behave? What was their motivation for survival?

As you prepare for your presentation, emphasize the fact that this is a true story. You might even ask the audience what their own breaking points have been. You might point out on a map all the places Elie was moved to, tell the distances, and explain how he was transported from place to place. Elie's will to survive was tremendous, even throughout his changing beliefs. How will you convey this to the class?

Name _____   Date _____

<h1 style="text-align:center">Unit Outline:</h1>

<h1 style="text-align:center">Night</h1>

<h2 style="text-align:center">by Elie Wiesel</h2>

Day 1:

1. Assign a role to each group member:
   (a) *Secretary:* Someone to record the group assignments and discussions.
   (b) *Taskmaster:* Someone to read instructions each day.
   (c) *Assignment Collector:* Someone to collect assignments and turn them in each day.
   (d) *Librarian:* Someone to get the books and return them each day.
   (e) *Activity Director:* Someone to organize group activities.

2. Identify group members who would like to read aloud.

3. Complete the Questionnaire sheet on your own. Upon completion, discuss your responses with your group. Why did you choose the items you did? Does your group have the same or differing opinions? Justify or defend your responses.*

4. The Librarian needs to collect the books for group members.

5. The Taskmaster will read the introductory material aloud to the group so that all group members will have a good idea of what will be expected during the unit.

6. If there's still time left in the class period, begin reading aloud.

Day 2:

1. Predict the events in *Night* by using the handout. Write your responses at the bottom of the handout.*

2. Read **aloud** p. 1 to the top of p. 12. These pages can be difficult to understand. Make sure you ask questions or look up words you do not understand. If you are really confused, ask your teacher for clarification.

3. Fill out Day 2 Section Summary/Title sheet. Make sure you read the directions carefully. This can be a group effort; however, each group member will be responsible for his/her own paper. This assignment will be turned in when you are finished reading the book.

4. This book has a lot of characters, and a character chart will help you keep track of who is who. Make a chart of important characters using your own paper. Include the following information:
   (a) name
   (b) physical description (height, weight, hair color, eye color, etc.)
   (c) profession, hobbies, and interests
   (d) You might include their relationships to the main character.

   Each student will turn in a final, polished copy at the end of the unit, so you should work on a rough draft during the reading and rewrite your chart when you have completed the book.

Day 3:

1. Read from p. 12 to the middle of p. 24 ("an endless night . . .").

2. Fill out Section Summary/Title worksheet. If necessary, add to the character chart.

---

* All group discussions must be written up by the Secretary and turned in at the completion of the discussion.

33 *Holocaust Literature:*
Study Guides to 12 Stories of Courage

Unit Outline: *Night*

Day 4:   1. Read from p. 24 to the bottom of p. 31.

2. Fill out Section Summary/Title worksheet. Add to your character sheet.

3. Dialogue worksheet. (When everyone in the group is finished, check with your teacher for the page number so you may check your answers.) Make sure you follow the directions . . . several of these worksheets require you to rewrite the passage in final form. Turn in your assignment when finished.

Day 5:   1. Read from p. 31 to p. 41 (middle of the page).

2. Fill out Section Summary/Title worksheet. Add to your character chart if necessary.

3. Group discussison:*
Scan the material on pp. 27–41 and then answer the following questions. Did you all agree? Who thought what? Show your proof with page references if possible.

(a) Justify Elie's reaction when his father was struck savagely by Idek. Why did he act that way? How did you feel after reading that paragraph?

(b) Why did the man talk to Elie and his father about their ages? Why was it significant?

(c) At what point did Elie's life turn into one long night? What are the events he will never forget?

(d) What is Elie's one goal from the start when they reach the camp and he is separated from his mother and sister?

(e) How did the prisoners feel about the relatives who were no longer with them?

(f) Emotionally, what is happening to Elie? How are his beliefs changing? Do you agree with them? Do you understand?

Day 6:   1. Read from p. 41 to the middle of p. 52.

2. Complete Section Summary/Title worksheet. Add to your character chart if necessary.

3. Complete Day 6: Ellipses worksheet. Turn in when finished.

Day 7:   1. Read from the middle of p. 52 to p. 62.

2. Complete Section Summary/Title worksheet. Add to your character chart if necessary.

3. Group discussion: Explain Elie's meaning when he says after the hanging of the youth from Warsaw that "The soup tasted excellent that evening," yet after the pipal (the angel) was hanged, "the soup tasted of corpses." Did he mean that the soup was made from corpses? What type of figurative language is this? Why, from a writer's point of view, did he choose this positioning of one statement after another, side by side? What did you learn from this?*

Day 8:   1. Read from the top of p. 63 to top break of p. 72.

2. Complete Section Summary/Title worksheet. Add to your character chart if necessary.

3. Complete Simile worksheet. Turn in when finished.

Day 9:   1. Read from the top of p. 72 to the end of p. 80.

2. Complete Section Summary/Title worksheet. Update character chart.

---

* All group discussions must be written up by the Secretary and turned in at the completion of the discussion.

© 1997 J. Weston Walch, Publisher   34   *Holocaust Literature:*
Study Guides to 12 Stories of Courage

Name _____   Date _____

Unit Outline: *Night*

Day 10:   1. Read from p. 81 to p. 98.

2. Complete Section Summary/Title worksheet. Update character chart if necessary

3. Complete Copy Change assignment. Read the directions carefully. Because this assignment may take a little longer to complete, you may have to finish it at home. Be sure to rewrite your finished product on notebook paper in paragraph form.

Day 11:   1. Finish the book, reading to p. 109.

2. Complete and turn in your Section Summary/Title worksheet. Complete your rough draft of your character chart. Create a final copy, due on Day 13.

3. Complete the Cause and Effect flowchart. The teacher will provide instructions. Turn in when finished.

Day 12:   1. Group discussion: The human will to survive is tremendous. Have you ever run two miles? Can you imagine trying to run two miles on a snowy, winter day? How about when you were hungry? Discuss reasons for these people to survive running not two, but 40 miles when they were malnourished and had virtually no energy because of lack of food. What was their motivation? Could you do it? Why or why not? What motivation would you need? Next refer to p. 109. Read aloud beginning with "Our first act . . .". Why did Elie not think of revenge? Would you feel the same? Discuss this with your group.*

2. Discuss the Importance Chart as a group and have the Secretary record the group consensus to turn in.

3. Begin working on the handout "Never Shall I . . ."

Day 13:   1. Complete all unfinished assignments.

2. Begin working on Holocaust Literature handout. The teacher will provide instructions. Use the Holocaust Essay Form for your final copy of the written assignment.

Days 14–17: 1. The Taskmaster will read the instructions from the Class Presentation sheet. The group should formulate some ideas, with the Secretary taking notes. During these days, your group should be putting together your presentation and related assignments, as well as rehearsing for the class presentation.

Determine who will be responsible for what parts. Before you present, you will need to turn in a paper neatly written in ink with all of your names in the heading that will outline the responsibilities for each group member. Each member will be graded individually for his/her part in the presentation.*

Days 18–20: Class presentations. There will be a five-question quiz at the end of each presentation.

---

* All group discussions must be written up by the Secretary and turned in at the completion of the discussion.

35   *Holocaust Literature:*
Study Guides to 12 Stories of Courage

Name _____   Date _____

Night

By Elie Wiesel
Day 1: Questionnaire

Read the following questions and determine for yourself the answers you think are best. You may choose two or three items per question.

1. *What words best describe **prejudice**?*

   _____ obstinate   _____ single-minded   _____ biased

   _____ forceful   _____ conceited   _____ ignorant

   _____ stubborn   _____ poor   _____ wealthy

   _____ judgmental   _____ unloved   _____ opinionated

2. *What do you think causes a person to become prejudiced?*

   _____ He/She was just born that way.

   _____ His/Her parents taught him/her to be that way by their example.

   _____ He/She observes incidents on television and at school.

   _____ He/She lives in an area where he/she is in the minority.

   _____ He/She lives in an area where he/she is in the vast majority.

   _____ He/She has been the victim in a race-related incident.

   _____ He/She has been the victim in an ethnic-related incident.

   _____ His/Her religion teaches supremacy of one race over another.

3. *How would you recognize a prejudiced person?*

   _____ From the way he/she lives.

   _____ From his/her facial expressions.

   _____ From his/her actions toward athletes, comedians, or politicians of different ethnic, racial, or religious backgrounds.

   _____ From the way he/she teases, taunts people.

4. *How would you cure a prejudiced person?*

   _____ With love and kindness, understanding.

   _____ With reasoning and knowledge.

   _____ By giving him/her a taste of his/her own medicine.

   _____ By getting someone to beat or frighten him/her.

   _____ There is no cure.

Name _____ Date _____

Night
Summaries and Titles

Directions:

1. Each member of the group will keep track of each of the section summaries in the book and turn in this assignment at the end of the reading. **Each of you will also be responsible for predicting future events based on what you have just read.**

2. After reading each day, look back over the pages read and think about what you might title the reading for that day if you were the author of the book. After the group members have individually decided on chapter titles, have a group discussion on why the titles were given. Which title does the group agree is the most accurate?

	Section Summary and Prediction	**Section Title**
Day 2 Pages read:		Why?
Day 3 Pages read:		Why?
Day 4 Pages read:		Why?
Day 5 Pages read:		Why?

(continued)

Holocaust Literature:
Study Guides to 12 Stories of Courage

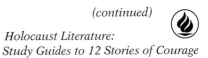

Night
Summaries and Titles *(continued)*

	Section Summary and Prediction	**Section Title**
Day 6 Pages read:		Why?
Day 7 Pages read:		Why?
Day 8 Pages read:		Why?
Day 9 Pages read:		Why?
Day 10 Pages read:		Why?
Day 11 Pages read:		Why?

Night
Day 2: Predicting the Outcome

In your group, discuss the following questions and record your discussion on this sheet. At the end of the discussion, hand in this sheet with your answers. Write a paragraph predicting what you think this book will be about.

1. Define the word *night*.

2. Why would the author use this word to title his work?

3. Considering the definitions, what does your group think may happen or may be the major theme of this book?

Night
Day 4: Dialogue

Punctuate the following passage correctly for dialogue. Remember that with each new speaker there is a new paragraph. If this is homework because your group did not complete the daily assignments, have it ready to turn in at the beginning of class tomorrow. Rewrite it in ink in the space provided below, or use your own paper. Be careful to include the necessary commas, periods, and capitalization.

here kid how old are you it was one of the prisoners who asked me this I could not see his face but his voice was tense and weary i'm not quite fifteen yet no eighteen but i'm not I said fifteen fool listen to what I say then he questioned my father who replied fifty the other grew more furious than ever no not fifty forty do you understand eighteen and forty

Holocaust Literature:
Study Guides to 12 Stories of Courage

Night
Day 6: Ellipses

Wiesel's writing throughout the book is thought provoking and uses ellipses to show that words have been omitted or to indicate a pause in thought. What is an ellipsis? An ellipsis is three periods . . . used to show that one or more words have been omitted in a quotation, or to indicate a pause.

"Well, Dad, I . . . ah . . . ran out of gas . . . had two flat tires . . . and ah . . . there was a terrible snowstorm on the other side of town."

"I have a dream . . . they will not be judged by the color of their skin but by the content of their character."

Above are two examples of ellipsis, one for pausing and one for omission of words.

Your job is to find two ellipses used by Wiesel in *Night* and record them below, making sure they are in sentences of more than five words. Be sure to indicate the pages you found them on.

1.

2.

Next . . . write two sentences of your own: one where words are omitted, and the other where you want to pause. Be sure the sentences are *compound sentences,* and that they are *complete* and *interesting*.

1.

2.

Holocaust Literature:
Study Guides to 12 Stories of Courage

Night
Day 8: Similes

A good definition of a *simile* is a comparison of two things in which a word of comparison ("like" or "as") is used:

"Mr. Kosinski's eyes are **like** charging bulls when he is mad."

Find five similes in the book from the pages you have read. List each simile and the page where it appears.

How did the similes help you see and understand the character or situation? Were they valuable? Write three similes for three characters or situations dealing with the portion of the book you read for today. Which do you like better, Wiesel's or your own? Why?

Hand in your similes and your recorded discussion.

Name _____ Date _____

Night
Day 10: Copy Change Assignment

On p. 86 in *Night*, there is a description of Rabbi Eliahou:

The door of the shed opened. An old man appeared, his mustache covered with frost, his lips blue with cold. It was Rabbi Eliahou, the rabbi of a small Polish community. He was a very good man, well loved by everyone in the camp, even by the Kapos and the heads of the blocks. Despite the trials and privations, his face still shone with his inner purity. He was the only rabbi who was always addressed as "Rabbi" at Buna. He was like one of the old prophets, always in the midst of his people to comfort them. And, strangely, his words of comfort never provoked rebellion, they really brought peace."

Your assignment is to copy change this paragraph to describe someone you know well. It may be serious, it may be corny, but it must follow the pattern and it must make sense in order to warrant a grade. Here is an example that describes the vice principal of our school. This paragraph copies the pattern from the paragraph in *Night*, but changes the words to fit this person:

The door of the classroom opened. A man appeared, his face cheerful, his expression encouraging. It was Mr. Bell, the Vice Principal of Fairmont Junior High. He was a very fair man, well liked by everyone at school, even by the students and their parents. Despite the difficulties of his job, his attitude still remained positive and he was always trying to make a change in student behavior. He was the one who was addressed as the "singer" at Fairmont. He was always in the halls, trying to get students and teachers alike to sing the "I want to be a Fairmontian" song. And, strangely, his behavior never brought about rebellion, it merely brought smiles.

Write your copy change in ink and hand it in on a separate sheet of paper. Be sure to check your spelling and punctuation and by all means, have fun. If you are having a difficult time coming up with a copy change on your own, you can follow the pattern provided on the back by filling in the blanks with the appropriate words.

(over)

Night
Day 10: Copy Change Assignment *(continued)*

The _____ of the _____ . _____

his/her _____, his/her _____ .

It was _____ , the _____ of _____ .

He/She was _____, well _____ by everyone at/in _____ ,

even by _____ and _____ . Despite the _____ and

_____, his/her _____ still _____ . He/She

_____ who was always addressed as _____ .

He/She was _____, always in the _____

to _____ them. And, strangely, _____ his _____

of _____ never _____,

they really brought _____.

Night
Day 11: Cause and Effect

Show how the events in a story determine future events by filling in the squares with causes and effects from *Night*. Begin each sentence with *Since* or *Because*. When you begin a sentence with either of these two words, you create a complex sentence, and there needs to be a comma at the end of the first clause. The first one has been done for you.

Because Elie's family is Jewish, they are sent to live in a ghetto.

Since Elie's family is sent to live in a ghetto,

Holocaust Literature:
Study Guides to 12 Stories of Courage

Name _____   Date _____

Night
Day 12: Importance Chart

On the lines below, list the 10 events (in order of occurrence) that your group considers the most important events in the book. Then explain why.

1. _____ ,

   because _____ .

2. _____ ,

   because _____ .

3. _____ ,

   because _____ .

4. _____ ,

   because _____ .

5. _____ ,

   because _____ .

6. _____ ,

   because _____ .

7. _____ ,

   because _____ .

8. _____ ,

   because _____ .

9. _____ ,

   because _____ .

10. _____ ,

    because _____ .

Holocaust Literature:
Study Guides to 12 Stories of Courage

Night
Day 12: "Never Shall I . . ."

This assignment might be a challenge, but it may also be a great moment of expression for you. You will be creating a free verse poem or a list from your own memories. You will have two options, listed below. So that you can understand where this is coming from, refer to p. *ix* in the foreword and p. 32 in the text. You can see that Elie Wiesel has very strong feelings about that time in his life.

Choose one of the following to create a list or a poem about your own personal memories.

1. Brainstorm at least 10 things from your childhood that you will never forget. They may be happy times or sad times or a combination of both. Begin each line with "Never shall I forget . . ." and tell enough about that experience or event so that your reader will understand why you won't forget that moment in time. When you have at least 10 items, take the top five or seven that have the most meaning to you or that you like the best. Put those together to create a list or a free verse poem. In the last line, end with a thought or feeling as to why you will never forget those things. Use Elie's example to help you.

2. Think of one particular time in your life that you will never forget. It may be an extremely happy time or it may be a sad time. Now, free-write everything you can remember about that experience. Go through your senses (sight, smell, taste, touch, sound) and try to remember and describe each one.

   Now look back over what Elie wrote. See if you can take your memories and cut them into short, but meaningful sentences to show your true feelings. You might have to cut some parts out or add more description. A good writer must play with words before the final product can be powerful.

   Use your feelings . . . express yourself. Who knows, you too may become a great writer.

47

Holocaust Literature:
Study Guides to 12 Stories of Courage

Name _____   Date _____

Night
Grading Sheet

Assignment	Possible Points	Student ✓	Teacher ✓	Points
1. Questionnaire Responses				
2. Day 2: Predicting the Outcome				
3. Day 4: Dialogue				
4. Day 5: Group Discussion				
5. Day 6: Ellipses				
6. Day 7: Group Discussion				
7. Day 8: Similes				
8. Day 10: Copy Change				
9. Section Summaries/Titles				
10. Day 11: Cause and Effect				
11. Day 12: Group Discussion				
12. Day 12: Importance Chart				
13. Day 12: "Never Shall I . . ."				
14. Day 13: Character Chart				
15. Day 13: Holocaust Literature				
16. Day 13: Holocaust Essay				
17. Class Presentation				
18. Character Bag				
19. Class Quizzes				
20. Group Participation				
			Total Pts.	
			Grade	

Holocaust Literature:
Study Guides to 12 Stories of Courage

The Hiding Place

by Corrie ten Boom

The Hiding Place

by Corrie ten Boom

To the Student

Imagine having your life changed because of war. Instead of sleeping peacefully, you worry about air raids and bombs exploding during the night. Your friends suddenly become divided because of religious beliefs, and some of the people you see daily are beaten, taken away, or even killed before your very eyes! Could you stand by and watch this taking place? Would you run away? Would you help those people whose lives were at stake, thus risking your life?

There were many heroes of World War II who risked their lives to save others. Corrie ten Boom was one of those heroes. The story you are about to read took place in Holland. Corrie and her family were simple people who worked at their watch shop located on the first floor of their house and followed their Christian faith. As they watched the German invasion in their town of Haarlem, they witnessed the persecution of many of their Jewish friends. These events led them to the decision that they could help by becoming a part of the "underground" community.

The people of the underground risked their lives by doing illegal things: stealing ration cards, illegally obtaining radios, and moving around after curfew. But most importantly they helped to hide Jews. In making their decision, Corrie ten Boom's family put their own lives at stake as well as the lives of anyone associated with the watch shop.

As you prepare for your presentation, emphasize the fact that Corrie ten Boom and her family were *not* Jewish. Be sure to explain their involvement in the underground, and explain some of the things the underground did to help the Jews. Also explain how Corrie survived. If she hadn't had a strong religious background, do you think the story might have been the same?

Unit Outline:

The Hiding Place

by Corrie ten Boom

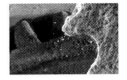

Day 1:

1. Assign a role to each group member:

   (a) *Secretary:* Someone to record the group assignments and discussions. In record-ing the discussions, the Secretary should describe the general discussion—who thought what—and then describe how the discussion ended. Was there a consensus?

   (b) *Taskmaster:* Someone to read instructions each day.

   (c) *Assignment Collector:* Someone to collect assignments and turn them in each day.

   (d) *Librarian:* Someone to get the books and return them each day.

   (e) *Activity Director:* Someone to organize group activities.

2. Identify group members who would like to read aloud.

3. Complete the Questionnaire sheet on your own. Upon completion, discuss your responses with your group. Why did you choose the items you did? Does your group have the same or differing opinions? Justify or defend your responses.*

4. The Librarian needs to collect the books for group members.

5. The Taskmaster will read the introductory material aloud to the group so that all group members will have a good idea of what will be expected during the unit.

6. If there's still time left in the class period, begin reading aloud.

Day 2:

1. Skip the Preface and read pp. 1–24 ("Mondays . . .").

2. Fill out Day 2 Section Summary/Title sheet. Make sure you read the directions care-fully. This can be a group effort; however, each group member will be responsible for his/her own paper. This assignment will be turned in when you are finished reading the book.

3. This book has a lot of characters, and a character chart will help you keep track of who is who. Make a chart of the important characters using your own paper. Include the following information:

   (a) name

   (b) physical description (height, weight, hair color, eye color, etc.)

   (c) profession, hobbies, and interests

   (d) You might include their relationship to the main character.

   You will each be turning in a final, polished copy at the end of the unit, so you should work on a rough draft during the reading and rewrite your chart when you have completed the novel.

Day 3:

1. Read from pp. 24–45.

2. Fill out Section Summary/Title worksheet. If necessary, add to the character chart.

---

* All group discussions must be written up by the Secretary and turned in at the completion of the discussion.

Unit Outline: *The Hiding Place*

3. Group discussion: What is your impression of the ten Boom family? What do you know about them so far? Discuss what kind of family Corrie comes from. Also, why does the author use so much foreshadowing? (If you are unfamiliar with the term, find your classroom literature book, and look in the glossary located at the back to find the definition.) This discussion should be recorded on your own paper and turned in when completed.*

By now you have noticed that The Hiding Place *is one of the longer books. You must keep up with the reading or you will find yourself falling behind. The book may be available for checkout after school if you find yourself in this predicament. It is important that each member follows the assigned schedule so that the daily activities (such as group discussions) can be completed on the assigned date. Many of the assignments may be taken home and completed there.*

Day 4:
1. Read pp. 46–69 ("We talked often . . .").
2. Fill out Section Summary/Title worksheet. Add to your character sheet.
3. The characters in this novel are optimistic, religious people. They use many of their past experiences, biblical teachings, and education to help themselves survive, and they refer to them throughout the book. Read the preface starting on p. *xii*. In the last complete paragraph, Corrie stated, "This is what the past is for! Every experience God gives us, every person He puts in our lives is the perfect preparation for the future that only He can see!"

   Your group will be responsible for creating a "Life's Lessons" handbook. In it, you will creatively keep track of the lessons Corrie and her family frequently state. You must also document who said what and on which page. You might put the lessons in a recipe file, book form, a journal—you decide. This assignment will be due when you're finished reading the book.

Day 5:
1. Read pp. 69–88 (end of chapter).
2. Fill out Section Summary/Title worksheet. Add to your character chart if necessary.

Day 6:
1. Read pp. 89–108 (end of chapter).
2. Complete Section Summary/Title worksheet. Add to your character chart if necessary.
3. Spelling and Punctuation worksheet. When all group members have completed the worksheet, ask your teacher for the page number so that you may check your work. Turn in when finished. *Follow directions carefully. Most assignments require that the corrected passage be rewritten in ink.*

Day 7:
1. Read pp. 109–131.
2. Complete Section Summary/Title worksheet. Add to your character chart if necessary.

Day 8:
1. Read from pp. 132 to the break on p. 152 ("one evening . . .").
2. Complete Section Summary/Title worksheet. Add to your character chart if necessary.

---

* All group discussions must be written up by the Secretary and turned in at the completion of the discussion.

Unit Outline: *The Hiding Place*

3. Group discussion: What role does religion play in the ten Booms' lives? Do people need to believe in some outside force to get along in life? Explain. What did Corrie's vision have to do with their getting caught? How has the ten Booms' faith allowed them to survive? Go back to your definition of foreshadowing, and discuss any examples you have found. Again, how does foreshadowing add to the story? Why does the author continue to use this literary device? Predict what will happen to the group.*

Day 9:
1. Read pp. 152–175.
2. Complete Section Summary/Title worksheet. Update character chart.
3. Complete Dialogue worksheet. When all group members have completed the worksheet, ask your teacher for the page number so you can correct your work. Turn in when finished.

Day 10:
1. Read from p. 176 to the break at the top of p. 199 ("They started . . .").
2. Complete Section Summary/Title worksheet. Update character chart if necessary

Day 11:
1. Read pp. 199–220 (end of chapter).
2. Complete Section Summary/Title worksheet. Update character chart if necessary.
3. Complete the Cause and Effect flowchart. The teacher will provide instructions. Turn in when finished.

Day 12:
1. Read from p. 221 to the end of book, p. 241.
2. Complete and turn in your Section Summary/Title worksheet. Complete your rough draft of your character chart. Create a final copy, due on Day 13.
3. Discuss the Importance Chart as a group and have the Secretary record the group consensus to turn in.

Day 13:
1. Complete all unfinished assignments.
2. Begin working on Holocaust Literature handout. The teacher will provide instructions. Use the Holocaust Essay Form for your final copy of the written assignment.

Days 14–17:
1. The Taskmaster will read the instructions from the Class Presentation sheet. The group should formulate some ideas, with the Secretary taking notes. During these days, your group should be putting together your presentation and related assignments, as well as rehearsing for the class presentation.

Determine who will be responsible for what parts. Before you present, you will need to turn in a paper neatly written in ink with all of your names in the heading that will outline the responsibilities for each group member. Each member will be graded individually for his/her part in the presentation.*

Days 18–20: Class presentations. There will be a five-question quiz at the end of each presentation.

---

* All group discussions must be written up by the Secretary and turned in at the completion of the discussion.

Name _____ Date _____

The Hiding Place
by Corrie ten Boom
Day 1: Questionnaire

Read the following questions and determine for yourself the answers you think are best. You may choose two or three items per question.

1. *What words best describe **prejudice**?*

    _____ obstinate   _____ single-minded   _____ biased

    _____ forceful   _____ conceited   _____ ignorant

    _____ stubborn   _____ poor   _____ wealthy

    _____ judgmental   _____ unloved   _____ opinionated

2. *What do you think causes a person to become prejudiced?*

    _____ He/She was just born that way.

    _____ His/Her parents taught him/her to be that way by their example.

    _____ He/She observes incidents on television and at school.

    _____ He/She lives in an area where he/she is in the minority.

    _____ He/She lives in an area where he/she is in the vast majority.

    _____ He/She has been the victim in a race-related incident.

    _____ He/She has been the victim in an ethnic-related incident.

    _____ His/Her religion teaches supremacy of one race over another.

3. *How would you recognize a prejudiced person?*

    _____ From the way he/she lives.

    _____ From his/her facial expressions.

    _____ From his/her actions toward athletes, comedians, or politicians of different ethnic, racial, or religious backgrounds.

    _____ From the way he/she teases, taunts people.

4. *How would you cure a prejudiced person?*

    _____ With love and kindness, understanding.

    _____ With reasoning and knowledge.

    _____ By giving him/her a taste of his/her own medicine.

    _____ By getting someone to beat or frighten him/her.

    _____ There is no cure.

54   *Holocaust Literature: Study Guides to 12 Stories of Courage*

Name _____   Date _____

The Hiding Place
Summaries and Titles

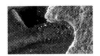

Directions:

1. Each member of the group will keep track of each of the section summaries in the book and turn in this assignment at the end of the reading. **Each of you will also be responsible for predicting future events based on what you have just read.**

2. After reading each day, look back over the pages read and think about what you might title the reading for that day if you were the author of the book. After the group members have individually decided on chapter titles, have a group discussion on why the titles were given. Which title does the group agree is the most accurate?

	Section Summary and Prediction	**Section Title**
Day 2 Pages read:		Why?
Day 3 Pages read:		Why?
Day 4 Pages read:		Why?
Day 5 Pages read:		Why?

(continued)

Name _____ Date _____

The Hiding Place
Summaries and Titles *(continued)*

	Section Summary and Prediction	**Section Title**
Day 6 Pages read:		Why?
Day 7 Pages read:		Why?
Day 8 Pages read:		Why?
Day 9 Pages read:		Why?
Day 10 Pages read:		Why?

(continued)

Holocaust Literature:
Study Guides to 12 Stories of Courage

The Hiding Place
Summaries and Titles *(continued)*

	Section Summary and Prediction	**Section Title**
Day 11 Pages read:		Why?
Day 12 Pages read:		Why?

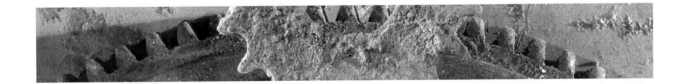

The Hiding Place
Day 6: Spelling and Punctuation

Read through the following excerpt from the novel, correcting spelling and adding punctuation where needed.

When you have edited this passage, **rewrite the paragraph correctly on your own paper.** When all group members have completed this assignment, ask your teacher for the page number so you may correct your work.

I tried again to protest but mr smit had forgotten I existed over the next few days he and his workmen where in and out of hour house constantly they never nocked at each visit eachman carryd in something tools in a folded newspaper a few bricks in a breifcase wood he exclaimed when I ventured to wonder if a wooden wall would not be easier to build wood sounds hollow hear it in a minute no no bricks the only thing for false walls

Holocaust Literature:
Study Guides to 12 Stories of Courage

The Hiding Place
Day 9: Dialogue

Puncuate the following passage correctly for dialogue. Remember that with each new speaker there is a new paragraph. If this is homework because your group did not complete the daily assignments, have it ready to turn in at the beginning of class tomorrow. When all group members have the assignment completed, you may ask your teacher for the correct page number so you may correct your work.

Rewrite the paragraph in ink using your own paper. Be careful to include the necessary commas, periods, and capitalization.

Miss ten Boom he said Welcome How do you do, Sir The chief had left his desk to shut the door behind me Do sit down he said I know all about you you know About your work The watchmaking you mean You're probably thinking more about my father's work than my own The chief smiled No I mean your 'other' work Ah then you're referring to my work with retarded children? Yes. Let me tell you about that— No miss ten boom the chief lowered his voice I am not talking about your work with retarded children I'm talking about still another work, and I want you to know that some of us here are in sympathy The chief was smiling broadly now Tentatively I smiled back Now miss ten boom he went on I have a request The chief sat down on the edge of his desk and looked at me steadily He dropped his voice until it was just audible he was he said working with the underground himself but an informer in the police department was leaking information to the Gestapo There's no way for us to deal with this man but to kill him.

The Hiding Place
Day 11: Cause and Effect

Show how the events in a story determine future events by filling in the squares with causes and effects from *The Hiding Place*. Begin each sentence with *Since* or *Because*. When you begin a sentence with either of these two words, you create a complex sentence, and there needs to be a comma at the end of the first clause. The first one has been done for you.

Because the ten Boom family had room in their home, they chose to build a hiding place to help Jews.

Because they chose to build a hiding place to help Jews,

Holocaust Literature:
Study Guides to 12 Stories of Courage

The Hiding Place
Day 12: Importance Chart

On the lines below, list the 10 events (in order of occurrence) that your group considers the most important events in the book. Then explain why.

1. _____ ,

   because _____ .

2. _____ ,

   because _____ .

3. _____ ,

   because _____ .

4. _____ ,

   because _____ .

5. _____ ,

   because _____ .

6. _____ ,

   because _____ .

7. _____ ,

   because _____ .

8. _____ ,

   because _____ .

9. _____ ,

   because _____ .

10. _____ ,

   because _____ .

Name _____   Date _____

The Hiding Place
Grading Sheet

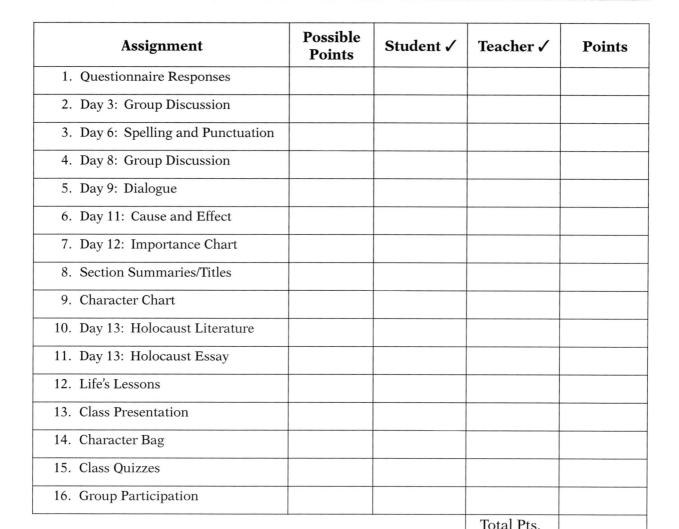

Assignment	Possible Points	Student ✓	Teacher ✓	Points
1. Questionnaire Responses				
2. Day 3: Group Discussion				
3. Day 6: Spelling and Punctuation				
4. Day 8: Group Discussion				
5. Day 9: Dialogue				
6. Day 11: Cause and Effect				
7. Day 12: Importance Chart				
8. Section Summaries/Titles				
9. Character Chart				
10. Day 13: Holocaust Literature				
11. Day 13: Holocaust Essay				
12. Life's Lessons				
13. Class Presentation				
14. Character Bag				
15. Class Quizzes				
16. Group Participation				
			Total Pts.	
			Grade	

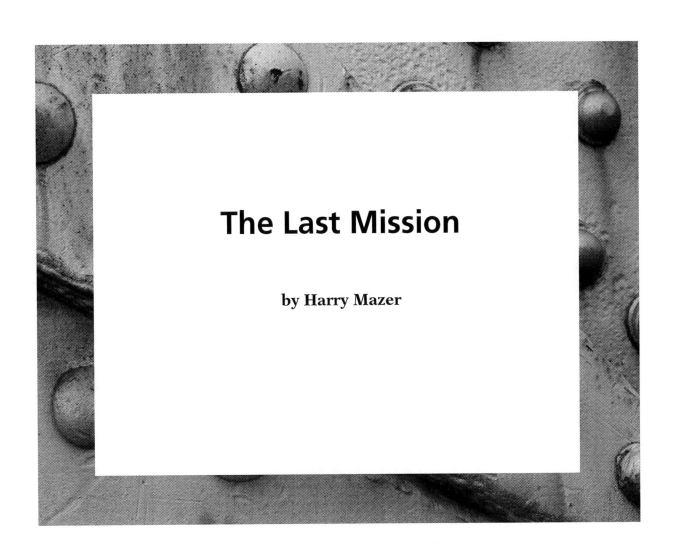

The Last Mission

by Harry Mazer

The Last Mission

by Harry Mazer

To the Student

Imagine finding out that some madman is wiping out millions of people—teenagers, children, and adults—just because of their religion. Your religion is the same and you are safe simply because you live in a different country. How would you feel? If you are like Jack Raab, you want to hunt this madman down and kill him.

Jack is the main character in Harry Mazer's fictional book. Jack is a 15-year-old boy living in New York City who dreams of being a hero. He sees his chance when his older brother avoids the draft because of an injury. Jack steals his brother's I.D. and lies his way into the U.S. Air Force.

Mazer creates realistic characters, showing the shock, grief, and suffering associated with World War II. Not only did the Jews suffer at the hands of Hitler, but many Americans did as well. Jack was a Jewish American, and Mazer shows his apprehension about being a Jew on enemy turf after his plane was shot down over Germany.

This novel does contain mature language as the author tries to present the concept of a young boy moving too quickly into adult situations. Only students with the maturity to handle this language should choose to read this novel. It has been included in this unit because of the American military perspective it provides. Mazer does an excellent job at capturing an American boy's rite of passage.

As you prepare for your presentation, consider the changes Jack goes through. He starts out thinking he will be able to go right in and kill Hitler, and he ends up with a mature ability to see the true meaning of war. The last chapter includes a very dramatic scene with Jack talking to the kids at his high school. (This scene might be a powerful one to read or act out for your presentation.) Be sure to explain the misery Jack encounters when he is on enemy soil. Are the Jews the only ones suffering because of this war?

Name _____ Date _____

Unit Outline:

The Last Mission

by Harry Mazer

Day 1:

1. Assign a role to each group member:

   (a) *Secretary:* Someone to record the group assignments and discussions. In recording the discussions, the Secretary should describe the general discussion—who thought what—and then describe how the discussion ended. Was there a consensus?

   (b) *Taskmaster:* Someone to read instructions each day and keep the group on task.

   (c) *Assignment Collector:* Someone to collect assignments and turn them in each day.

   (d) *Librarian:* Someone to get the books and return them each day. The Librarian will also complete any research required.

   (e) *Activity Director:* Someone to organize group activities.

2. Identify group members who would like to read aloud.

3. Complete the Questionnaire sheet on your own. Upon completion, discuss your responses with your group. Why did you choose the items you did? Does your group have the same or differing opinions? Justify or defend your responses.*

4. The Librarian needs to collect the books for group members.

5. The Taskmaster will read the introductory material aloud to the group so that all group members will have a good idea of what will be expected during the unit.

6. If there's still time left in the class period, browse through your books. Discuss and predict what you think this book will be like.*

Day 2:

1. As a group, read Harry Mazer's book dedication as well as Part 1 on pp. 5, 6, and 7. Predict Mazer's reasons for writing this book as well as predicting his background.*

2. Read Chapter 1 aloud—pp. 9–18.

3. Fill out Day 2 Section Summary/Title worksheet. Make sure you read the directions carefully. This can be a group effort; however, each group member will be responsible for his/her own paper. This assignment will be turned in when you are finished reading the book.

4. This book has a lot of characters, and a character chart will help you keep track of who is who. Make a chart of the important characters, using your own paper. Include the following information:

   (a) name (you might include their relationship to the main character)
   (b) physical description (height, weight, hair color, eye color, etc.)
   (c) profession, hobbies, and interests
   (d) what they have lost or what has been taken away from them

   Each of you will be turning in a final, polished copy at the end of the unit, so you should work on a rough draft during the reading and rewrite your chart when you have completed the book.

---

* All group discussions must be written up by the Secretary and turned in at the completion of the discussion.

Unit Outline: *The Last Mission*

Day 3:
1. Read Chapters 2 and 3. At this point your group may decide to read aloud or silently.
2. Complete Section Summary/Title worksheet for Day 3.
3. Add to your character chart if necessary.
4. Complete Ellipses worksheet.

Day 4:
1. Read Chapter 4.
2. Complete Section Summary/Title worksheet.
3. Add to your character chart if necessary.

Day 5:
1. Research the background on planes used during World War II. Identify the plane Jack flew in and have the Secretary take notes about that plane. Also explain anything else you might know about the planes flown during this war.*
2. Read Chapters 5 and 6.
3. Complete Section Summary/Title worksheet.
4. Add to your character chart if necessary.
5. Your group will be responsible for turning in a map showing as many of Jack's missions and journeys as possible. Your Librarian will want to find a map that will work for this, or someone may draw one. You need to have this map labeled with a key so that we can tell exactly where Jack flew from and where he flew to. Be creative. This will be due at the end of Day 13.

Day 6:
1. Read Chapters 7 and 8.
2. Complete Section Summary/Title worksheet.
3. Add to character chart if necessary.
4. Complete Description worksheet.

Day 7:
1. Read Chapters 9 and 10.
2. Complete Section Summary/Title worksheet.
3. Add to character chart if necessary.
4. Complete Copy Change assignment.

Day 8:
1. Read Chapters 11, 12, and 13.
2. Complete Section Summary/Title worksheet.
3. Add to character chart if necessary.
4. Group discussion: On your own paper, answer the following questions:
   (a) What are Jack's feelings about war and flying?
   (b) How have Jack's feelings changed regarding his missions and his companions? Have any of you ever felt that way about something?
   (c) What do you think it means to be an American? Why do so many foreigners work so hard to move to America? Do you think people still value and/or understand the freedoms we have as Americans? Why or why not? Explain each of your answers.

---

* All group discussions must be written up by the Secretary and turned in at the completion of the discussion.

Holocaust Literature:
Study Guides to 12 Stories of Courage

Unit Outline: *The Last Mission*

Day 9:   1. Read Chapters 14, 15, and 16.

2. Complete Section Summary/Title worksheet.

3. Add to character chart if necessary.

Day 10:   1. Read Chapters 17 and 18.

2. Complete Section Summary/Title worksheet.

3. Add to character chart if necessary.

4. Write a one-page letter from Jack to his parents explaining why he joined the army and what he experienced. Remember that he was close to his parents and could tell them just about anything. Also, consider the emotions Jack has gone through, leaving his family without saying goodbye and being away from them for the first time. There should be no question that Jack wrote the letter. This is due on Day 13.

Day 11:   1. Read Chapters 19 and 20.

2. Complete Section Summary/Title worksheet.

3. Add to the character chart if necessary.

4. Complete the Cause and Effect flowchart. The teacher will provide instructions. Turn in when finished.

Day 12:   1. Read Chapter 21.

2. Complete Section Summary/Title worksheet and turn in.

3. Complete rough draft of character chart. Write out your final copy in ink (or typed) and turn in.

4. As a group, complete the Importance Chart. You may use your Section Summary sheet or your observation list to help you. Complete your final copy of your character chart. This is due at the end of Day 13.

Day 13:   1. Begin working on Holocaust Literature handout. The teacher will provide instructions. Use the Holocaust Essay Form for your final copy of the written assignment.

2. Work on any unfinished assignments.

3. Turn in your letter from Jack, your group map, and your group Importance Chart.

Days 14–17: 1. Taskmaster will read the instructions from the project/presentation sheet. The group should formulate some ideas, with the Secretary taking notes. During these days, your group should be putting together your presentation and related assignments, as well as rehearsing for the class presentation.

Determine who will be responsible for what parts. Before you present, you will need to turn in a paper neatly written in ink with all of your names in the heading that will outline the responsibilities for each group member. Each member will be graded individually for his/her part in the presentation.*

Days 18–20:   Class presentations. There will be a five-question quiz at the end of each presentation.

---

* All group discussions must be written up by the Secretary and turned in at the completion of the discussion.

The Last Mission
by Harry Mazer
Day 1: Questionnaire

Read the following questions and determine for yourself the answers you think are best. You may choose two or three items per question.

1. *What words best describe **prejudice**?*

   _____ obstinate   _____ single-minded   _____ biased

   _____ forceful   _____ conceited   _____ ignorant

   _____ stubborn   _____ poor   _____ wealthy

   _____ judgmental   _____ unloved   _____ opinionated

2. *What do you think causes a person to become prejudiced?*

   _____ He/She was just born that way.

   _____ His/Her parents taught him/her to be that way by their example.

   _____ He/She observes incidents on television and at school.

   _____ He/She lives in an area where he/she is in the minority.

   _____ He/She lives in an area where he/she is in the vast majority.

   _____ He/She has been the victim in a race-related incident.

   _____ He/She has been the victim in an ethnic-related incident.

   _____ His/Her religion teaches supremacy of one race over another.

3. *How would you recognize a prejudiced person?*

   _____ From the way he/she lives.

   _____ From his/her facial expressions.

   _____ From his/her actions toward athletes, comedians, or politicians of
   different ethnic, racial, or religious backgrounds.

   _____ From the way he/she teases, taunts people.

4. *How would you cure a prejudiced person?*

   _____ With love and kindness, understanding.

   _____ With reasoning and knowledge.

   _____ By giving him/her a taste of his/her own medicine.

   _____ By getting someone to beat or frighten him/her.

   _____ There is no cure.

Name _____ Date _____

The Last Mission
Summaries and Titles

Directions:

1. Each member of the group will keep track of each of the section summaries in the book and turn in this assignment at the end of the reading. **Each of you will also be responsible for predicting future events based on what you have just read.**

2. After reading each day, look back over the pages read and think about what you might title the reading for that day if you were the author of the book. After the group members have individually decided on chapter titles, have a group discussion on why the titles were given. Which title does the group agree is the most accurate?

	Section Summary and Prediction	**Section Title**
Day 2 Pages read:		Why?
Day 3 Pages read:		Why?
Day 4 Pages read:		Why?
Day 5 Pages read:		Why?

(continued)

Holocaust Literature:
Study Guides to 12 Stories of Courage

Name _____   Date _____

The Last Mission
Summaries and Titles *(continued)*

	Section Summary and Prediction	**Section Title**
Day 6 Pages read:		Why?
Day 7 Pages read:		Why?
Day 8 Pages read:		Why?
Day 9 Pages read:		Why?
Day 10 Pages read:		Why?

(continued)

Holocaust Literature:
Study Guides to 12 Stories of Courage

The Last Mission
Summaries and Titles *(continued)*

	Section Summary and Prediction	**Section Title**
Day 11 Pages read:		Why?
Day 12 Pages read:		Why?

Holocaust Literature:
Study Guides to 12 Stories of Courage

Name _____   Date _____

The Last Mission
Day 3: Ellipses

Mazer's writing thoughout the book uses ellipses to show that words have
been omitted or to indicate a pause in thought. What is an ellipsis? An ellipsis is
three periods . . . used to show that one or more words have been omitted in a
quotation, or to indicate a pause.

"Well, Dad, I . . . ah . . . ran out of gas . . . had two flat tires . . . and ah . . . there
was a terrible snowstorm on the other side of town."

"I have a dream . . . . they will not be judged by the color of their skin but by
the content of their character."

Above are two examples of ellipsis, one for pausing and one for omittance
of words. Your job is to find two ellipses used by Mazer in *The Last Mission* and
record them below, making sure they are in sentences of more than five words.
Be sure to indicate the pages you found them on.

1.

2.

Next . . . write two sentences of your own: one where words are omitted,
and the other where you want to pause. Be sure the sentences are *compound
sentences,* and that they are *complete* and *interesting.*

1.

2.

The Last Mission
Day 6: Description

Harry Mazer doesn't use a lot of detailed description in his writing. Read the following paragraph and you will notice that the images are not as clear as they could be:

> Late in the day they stopped near a one-room schoolhouse. Soldiers were bivouacked[†] around the school. Willy went off, and Karl settled near Jack and Stan with his rifle across his knees. He took a loaf of black[††] bread and a chunk of cheese from the rucksack. Jack couldn't bear watching Karl eat, and he couldn't tear his eyes away from the food.

Your assignment is to add description to this paragraph so that the reader is better able to visualize the scene. Remember, adjectives and adverbs often help to make writing more descriptive. Consider the following: What exactly does the area look like? the schoolhouse itself? How were the soldiers encamped around it? Where did Willy go? Was he tired? happy? How about Karl and Stan? What kind of gun was it? Was Jack hungry? You should have a good idea of what to add. Too much is better than not enough.

The final copy should be on loose-leaf paper and written in ink.

[†] A temporary encampment often in an unsheltered area.
[††]Black bread is a type of bread; like wheat, white, etc.

The Last Mission
Day 7: Copy Change Assignment

This paragraph is found on p. 103:

Jack curled his toes in the insulated boots. Inside his helmet he could hear the whisper of his breath, each breath separate and hissing. And beyond the hissing, the constant high whining rush of the wind and the engines. He raised his voice so it matched the sound outside his head, wailing, singing his high monotonous song.

Assignment

In your mind, imagine a time when you were nervous or apprehensive about something. You might have been with friends, family or by yourself. Whatever you decide upon, it must be a situation that you actually experienced. For me, I remember going to my first dance when I was in seventh grade. I was so afraid that the ninth-graders wouldn't let me in or that I wouldn't be asked to dance. To make matters worse, my mom bought me these geeky new shoes to wear and I thought everyone would laugh at me when I walked in.

I have taken Harry Mazer's paragraph and **copied** the pattern of words, but **changed** it so my experience at the dance fits.

I curled my toes in my shiny new shoes. Inside my head I could hear the rapid beating of my heart, each beat loud and pounding. And beyond the pounding, the constant loud booming of the bass and the kids dancing. I raised my voice to my friend standing next to me so that it matched the sound outside my head, yelling in my frightened, whining voice.

You can use the pattern on the next page to help you come up with ideas. Rewrite the final copy in ink on loose-leaf paper.

(continued)

The Last Mission
Day 7: Copy Change Assignment *(continued)*

(Person) _____ ed _____ _____ in the

_____ _____ . Inside _____ _____

(person) could hear the _____ _____ _____,

each _____ _____ and

_____ (ing). And beyond the _____ (ing),

the constant _____ _____ (ing) of the _____

and the _____. (Person) raised _____

_____ so it matched the _____ _____

_____ _____, _____ (ing), _____ (ing)

_____ _____.

Holocaust Literature:
Study Guides to 12 Stories of Courage

The Last Mission
Day 11: Cause and Effect

Show how the events in a story determine future events by filling in the squares with causes and effects from *The Last Mission.* Begin each sentence with *Since* or *Because.* When you begin a sentence with either of these two words, you create a complex sentence, and there needs to be a comma at the end of the first clause. The first one has been done for you.

Because Jack wanted Hitler dead, he took his brother's birth certificate and joined the military.

Since Jack took his brother's birth certificate and joined the military,

Holocaust Literature:
Study Guides to 12 Stories of Courage

Name _____ Date _____

The Last Mission
Day 12: Importance Chart

On the lines below, list the 10 events (in order of occurrence) that your group considers the most important events in the book. Then explain why.

1. _____ ,

   because _____ .

2. _____ ,

   because _____ .

3. _____ ,

   because _____ .

4. _____ ,

   because _____ .

5. _____ ,

   because _____ .

6. _____ ,

   because _____ .

7. _____ ,

   because _____ .

8. _____ ,

   because _____ .

9. _____ ,

   because _____ .

10. _____ ,

   because _____ .

Holocaust Literature:
Study Guides to 12 Stories of Courage

Name _____ Date _____

The Last Mission
Grading Sheet

Assignment	Possible Points	Student ✓	Teacher ✓	Points
1. Questionnaire Responses				
2. Day 2: Group Discussion				
3. Day 3: Ellipses				
4. Day 6: Description				
5. Day 7: Copy Change				
6. Day 8: Group Discussion				
7. Day 11: Cause and Effect				
8. Section Summaries/Titles				
9. Character Chart				
10. Day 13: Holocaust Literature				
11. Day 13: Holocaust Essay				
12. Letter from Jack				
13. Group Map				
14. Day 12: Importance Chart				
15. Character Bag				
16. Class Presentation				
17. Class Quizzes				
18. Group Participation				
			Total Pts.	
			Grade	

Holocaust Literature:
Study Guides to 12 Stories of Courage

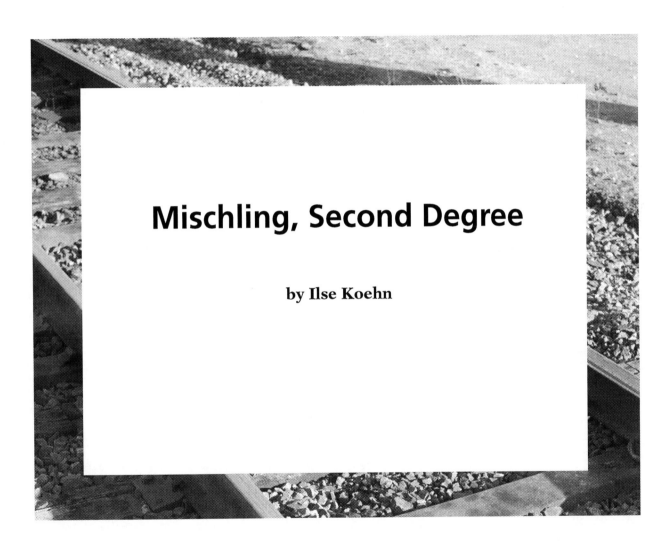

Mischling, Second Degree

by Ilse Koehn

Mischling, Second Degree

by Ilse Koehn

To the Student

This is a true story about Ilse Koehn, a young German girl who managed to survive the ravages of World War II. Her parents were "free thinkers," Germans who did not believe Hitler's propaganda. They weren't Jews, but Ilse had one grandparent who was a Jew, which made her a "Mischling, second degree." As such, she was likely to be persecuted along with all the other Jews living in Europe during the war. Her parents knew the situation, but Ilse did not; she only knew that what Hitler was doing was wrong, and that she could never be a Nazi youth. To make her life safer, Ilse's parents sent her to various camps along with other German girls. There, she would have to pretend to be a member of Nazi youth, an organization designed to "instill patriotism" in the children.

As you read this story, try to imagine what it would be like to have a war going on in your own country. Imagine what it might be like if a man like Hitler took over the United States and you were forced to leave your home at a very young age to go and live in camps with other children. Bombs, food shortages, and shootings would become an everyday occurrence. You might, then, be able to understand the hysteria of even the non-Jewish population as life slowly became an eerie nightmare.

When it comes time to do your book presentation to the class, be sure to explain the classification system for Jews. Koehn explains it clearly in the first chapter. Also, since Ilse moved around so much during the war, it might also be helpful to show the students on a map all the places where Ilse was sent while the war was going on.

We usually think that life was awful only for the Jewish people during World War II, but when you read this story, you'll find out that *everybody* suffered.

     Holocaust Literature:
Study Guides to 12 Stories of Courage

Unit Outline:

Mischling, Second Degree

by Ilse Koehn

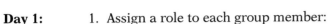

Day 1: 1. Assign a role to each group member:

  (a) *Secretary:* Someone to record the group assignments and discussions. In recording the discussions, the Secretary should describe the general discussion—who thought what—and then describe how the discussion ended. Was there a consensus?

  (b) *Taskmaster:* Someone to read instructions each day and keep the group on task.

  (c) *Assignment Collector:* Someone to make sure all assignments get turned in each day.

  (d) *Librarian:* Someone to get the books and return them each day. The Librarian will also complete any research required.

  (e) *Activity Director:* Someone to organize group activities.

  2. Identify group members who would like to read aloud.

  3. Complete the Questionnaire sheet on your own. Upon completion, discuss your responses with your group. Why did you choose the items you did? Does your group have the same or differing opinions? Justify or defend your responses on the back of your paper.*

  4. The Librarian needs to get the books at this point.

  5. The Taskmaster will read the introductory material aloud to the group so that all group members will have a good idea of what will be expected during the unit.

  6. If there's still time left in the class period, begin reading aloud.

Day 2: 1. Skip the foreword and read Chapter 1 and into Chapter 2 to p. 17 at the break.

  2. Fill out Day 2 Section Summary/Title. This can be a group effort; however, each group member will be responsible for his/her own paper. This assignment will be turned in when you're finished reading the book.

  3. Group discussion: What is your first impression of Ilse's father? her mother? her father's mother? her mother's parents?*

  4. As a group, discuss the names Ilse uses for her family members. Give an English equivalent and then make Ilse's family tree. Since the Secretary recorded the group discussion, have the Librarian write it up and turn it in either today or tomorrow.

Day 3: 1. Read the rest of Chapter 2, Chapter 3, and to the break on p. 35.

  2. Fill out Section Summary/Title for today's reading.

  3. Koehn writes this story with a consciousness of the history taking place in Germany at the time. Using the information she provides, begin making a historical chart or time line of what's happening during the war—probably broken down to month and year. Add to this time line daily and turn it in when you're finished reading.*

---

* All group discussions must be written up by the Secretary and turned in at the completion of the discussion.

Unit Outline: *Mischling, Second Degree*

Day 4:
    1. Read to the end of Chapter 6 on p. 58.

    2. Fill out Section Summary/Title and time line chart.

    3. Do Colon worksheet. Due today (or tomorrow if you don't finish in class).

Day 5:
    1. Read Chapter 7.

    2. Fill out Section Summary/Title and time line chart.

    3. For tomorrow, the Librarian needs to go to the library and find a map of Czechoslovakia that shows the cities that Ilse's been talking about. Bring back a copy for the group to see.

Day 6:
    1. Read Chapter 8, and to the break on p. 101.

    2. Fill out Section Summary/Title and time line chart.

    3. See if you can find Radoczowitz and the island of Ruegen on the map that the Librarian brought to class.

Day 7:
    1. Read to the break on p. 121.

    2. Fill out Section Summary/Title and time line chart.

    3. Find Harrachsdorf on a map of Europe.

    4. Do the Dialogue assignment. (See handout.) You might not have time to work on this in class; if so, take it home and bring it back finished to turn in tomorrow.

Day 8:
    1. Read to the break on p. 144.

    2. Fill out Section Summary/Title and time line chart.

    3. Group activity: Go back and reread the last paragraph on p. 115 and the first paragraph on p. 116. If you don't know the meaning of the word *propaganda*, look it up in a dictionary. Then read the last section of p. 149. Since the Secretary has already recorded the discussion, have the Librarian record your answers to the following questions:

       (a) What is the purpose of propaganda?

       (b) Think of at least two examples of propaganda that is used today. Is this good or bad? Why?*

Day 9:
    1. Read to the end of the chapter on p. 168.

    2. Fill out Section Summary/Title and time line chart.

Day 10:
    1. Read to the break on p. 193.

    2. Fill out Section Summary/Title and time line chart.

Day 11:
    1. Read to the break on p. 216.

    2. Fill out Section Summary/Title and time line chart.

    3. Do the Cause and Effect flowchart.

---

* All group discussions must be written up by the Secretary and turned in at the completion of the discussion.

Unit Outline: *Mischling, Second Degree*

Day 12:   1. Read to the break on p. 230.

2. Fill out Section Summary/Title and time line chart.

3. Group discussion of the Importance Chart. Turn one in for the group.*

Day 13:   1. Read to the end of the book.

2. Fill in the last Section Summary/Title and time line chart* and turn them in.

3. Begin working on the Holocaust Literature handout. The teacher will provide instructions. Use the Holocaust Essay Form for your final copy of the written assignment.

Days 14–17:   1. Holocaust essay due.

2. Begin planning the presentation that will be given to the class. The Taskmaster will read the instructions from the Class Presentation sheet. The group should formulate some ideas, with the Secretary taking notes. During the next four days, your group should be putting together your presentation and related assignment, as well as rehearsing for the class presentation.

Determine who will be responsible for what parts. Before you present, you will need to turn in a paper neatly written in ink with all of your names in the heading that will outline the responsibilities for each group member. Each member will be graded individually for his/her part in the presentation.*

Days 18–20:   Class presentations. There will be a five-question quiz at the end of each presentation.

---

* All group discussions must be written up by the Secretary and turned in at the completion of the discussion.

Name _____   Date _____

Mischling, Second Degree
by Ilse Koehn
Day 1: Questionnaire

Read the following questions and determine for yourself the answers you think are best. You may choose two or three items from each group.

1. *What words best describe **prejudice**?*

   _____ obstinate   _____ single-minded   _____ biased

   _____ forceful   _____ conceited   _____ ignorant

   _____ stubborn   _____ poor   _____ wealthy

   _____ judgmental   _____ unloved   _____ opinionated

2. *What do you think causes a person to become prejudiced?*

   _____ He/She was just born that way.

   _____ His/Her parents taught him/her to be that way by their example.

   _____ He/She observes incidents on television and at school.

   _____ He/She lives in an area where he/she is in the minority.

   _____ He/She lives in an area where he/she is in the vast majority.

   _____ He/She has been the victim in a race-related incident.

   _____ He/She has been the victim in an ethnic-related incident.

   _____ His/Her religion teaches supremacy of one race over another.

3. *How would you recognize a prejudiced person?*

   _____ From the way he/she lives.

   _____ From his/her facial expressions.

   _____ From his/her actions toward athletes, comedians, or politicians of different ethnic, racial, or religious backgrounds.

   _____ From the way he/she teases, taunts people.

4. *How would you cure a prejudiced person?*

   _____ With love and kindness, understanding.

   _____ With reasoning and knowledge.

   _____ By giving him/her a taste of his/her own medicine.

   _____ By getting someone to beat or frighten him/her.

   _____ There is no cure.

Holocaust Literature:
Study Guides to 12 Stories of Courage

Name _____ Date _____

Mischling, Second Degree
Summaries and Titles

Directions:

1. Each member of the group will keep track of each of the section summaries in the book and turn in this assignment at the end of the reading. **Each of you will also be responsible for predicting future events based on what you have just read.**

2. After reading each day, look back over the pages read and think about what you might title the reading for that day if you were the author of the book. After the group members have individually decided on chapter titles, have a group discussion on why the titles were given. Which title does the group agree is the most accurate?

	Section Summary and Prediction	**Section Title**
Day 2 Pages read:		Why?
Day 3 Pages read:		Why?
Day 4 Pages read:		Why?
Day 5 Pages read:		Why?

(continued)

Name _____   Date _____

Mischling, Second Degree
Summaries and Titles *(continued)*

	Section Summary and Prediction	**Section Title**
Day 6 Pages read:		Why?
Day 7 Pages read:		Why?
Day 8 Pages read:		Why?
Day 9 Pages read:		Why?
Day 10 Pages read:		Why?

(continued)

Mischling, Second Degree
Summaries and Titles (continued)

	Section Summary and Prediction	**Section Title**
Day 11 Pages read:		Why?
Day 12 Pages read:		Why?
Day 13 Pages read:		Why?

Holocaust Literature:
Study Guides to 12 Stories of Courage

Mischling, Second Degree
Day 4: Colons

A colon is a punctuation mark that is used before a long quotation, an explanation, an example, or a series. It is also used as a stylistic tool to focus the reader's attention on what is to come.

The following sentences were taken from this novel, but the colons have been replaced by commas. Insert the colons where you think they belong. Then check your work by looking up the original sentences in the book.

1. Talk is scarce, last night's raid, the expected sugar delivery at the grocery.

2. "Tell you what, I'll exempt you from everything—all duties, everything but meals—so you can finish . . ."

3. Another event, Ruth's mother came for a visit.

4. The final touch in this glorious valley, the one thing that makes everything perfect, Mutti. Mutti is here.

5. They [tales of unbelievable atrocities] always end in a statement that sounds like a threat, "No upright German will ever allow himself to be taken alive by these brutal beasts."

6. Whatever you believe, one thing is certain, the front is coming close.

7. We've finally decided to confront Pfaffi, will we be going to Berlin?

8. Most important, we all know the one place to be during an air raid, any bunker.

9. When we get back to the house, we find an excited crowd in our kitchen, Eberhard, his mother, the Ruhls and most of the women who used to meet for coffee and cake.

10. We have another visitor, young Schmid, the only known Super-Nazi on our street.

Mischling, Second Degree
Day 7: Dialogue

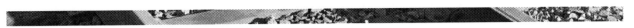

Rewrite the dialogue below, punctuating and paragraphing it correctly. (The speaker's name appears in italics, followed by a colon to indicate who is speaking; those names and colons do *not* belong in the dialogue.) When you are finished, ask the teacher for the page number so you can correct your work.

This is a conversation between Ilse and her roommate Sigrun. They are preparing for the room-decorating contest to "make the hotel feel more like home." Sigrun wants Ilse to do everything because she feels she's not as talented as Ilse.

Sigrun: I can't! I swear I can't. I'll ruin everything! Sigrun's voice is belligerent. *Ilse:* I plead: You can! You know you can. Why don't you let me show you? It's so easy! *Sigrun:* I don't want to. *Ilse:* But I can't do it all by myself! We'll never be finished in time! *Sigrun:* Oh, yes we will, and you *can* do it. I know you can. *Ilse:* But why won't you help? It's the room that wins, not one of us individually! *Sigrun:* I know! But I can't do this sort of thing and don't want to. I'll do all the cleaning, all your shoes too, keep the closet neat, everything for three months, if you do all this stuff and don't tell anyone. *Ilse, narrated:* I am dumbfounded. *Spoken:* You are crazy! Why would you want to do all the dirty stuff, and for three whole months? And what am I supposed to do while you clean? *Sigrun:* Sit and read or draw, comes her reply. That's what you like to do best anyway.

_____

_____

_____

_____

_____

_____

_____

_____

_____

(continued)

Mischling, Second Degree
Day 7: Dialogue *(continued)*

_____

_____

_____

_____

_____

_____

_____

_____

_____

_____

_____

_____

_____

_____

_____

_____

_____

_____

_____

_____

_____

_____

_____

_____

Mischling, Second Degree
Day 11: Cause and Effect

Show how the events in a story determine future events by filling in the squares with causes and effects from *Mischling, Second Degree*. Begin each sentence with *Since* or *Because*. When you begin a sentence with either of these two words, you create a complex sentence, and there needs to be a comma at the end of the first clause. The first one has been done for you.

Because Ilse's parents fear that the Nazis will harm Ilse because of her Jewish heritage, they send her to live with her other grandmother.

Since she lives with her other grand-mother,

Holocaust Literature:
Study Guides to 12 Stories of Courage

Mischling, Second Degree
Day 12: Importance Chart

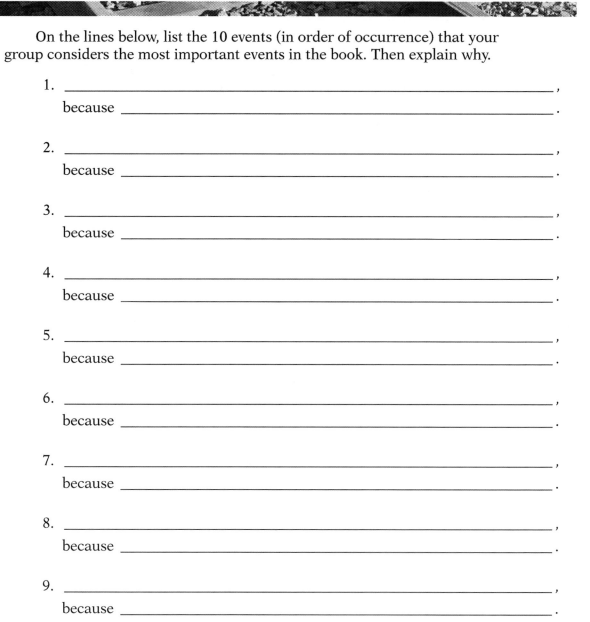

On the lines below, list the 10 events (in order of occurrence) that your group considers the most important events in the book. Then explain why.

1. _____ ,

   because _____ .

2. _____ ,

   because _____ .

3. _____ ,

   because _____ .

4. _____ ,

   because _____ .

5. _____ ,

   because _____ .

6. _____ ,

   because _____ .

7. _____ ,

   because _____ .

8. _____ ,

   because _____ .

9. _____ ,

   because _____ .

10. _____ ,

   because _____ .

Holocaust Literature:
Study Guides to 12 Stories of Courage

Name _____   Date _____

Mischling, Second Degree
Grading Sheet

Assignment	Possible Points	Student ✓	Teacher ✓	Points
1. Questionnaire Responses				
2. Day 2: Group Discussion				
3. Day 2: Family Tree				
4. Day 4: Colons				
5. Day 7: Dialogue				
6. Day 8: Group Activity				
7. Day 11: Cause and Effect				
8. Day 12: Importance Chart				
9. Section Summaries/Titles				
10. Time Line Chart				
11. Day 13: Holocaust Literature				
12. Day 13: Holocaust Essay				
13. Character Bag				
14. Class Presentation				
15. Class Quizzes				
16. Group Participation				
			Total Pts.	
			Grade	

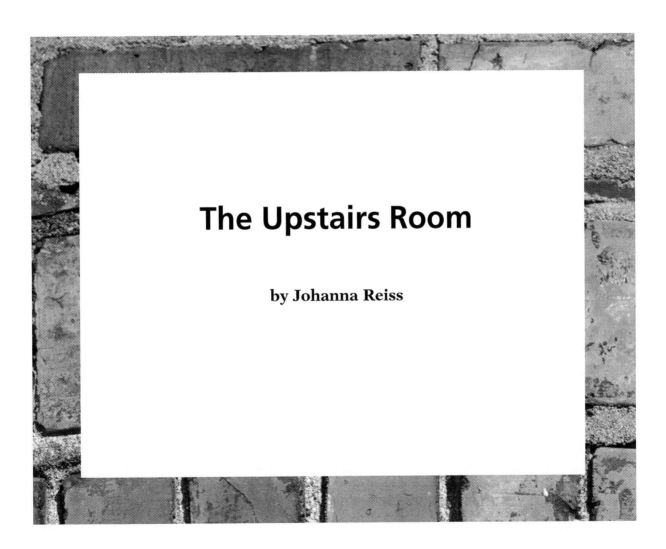

The Upstairs Room

by Johanna Reiss

The Upstairs Room

by Johanna Reiss

To the Student

Imagine being forced into staying inside, not for a day or two, but for a year or two! Many European Jews were forced into hiding in order to avoid being sent to concentration camps during World War II. Annie de Leeuw was 10 years old when she and her sister Sini had to leave their parents to hide in the upstairs room of a farmhouse.

For two years Annie was separated from her parents while waiting for the war to be over. A German family was kind enough to hide both Annie and Sini in their home. While they were kind to take them in, the pressure of the war and the confined space created an atmosphere of tension and heartache. *The Upstairs Room* is Johanna Reiss's own account of the experiences and feelings she went through during this difficult era.

As you are reading this book, try to think what you would do if you were ever forced into hiding. Could **you** handle the feeling that at any time you could be turned in to the Nazis and sent to an extermination camp? Could you remain calm and quiet in a two-foot space for over an hour? And would you be able to learn to live with strangers who harbor some resentment towards you because by hiding you, they are putting their own lives at stake?

As you prepare for your presentation, make the story come alive for the class by showing the amount of space Annie and Sini had when they hid in the closet. Explain some of the problems they encountered and how some things we take for granted were difficult for them. Also consider the other people involved in World War II. The Jews weren't the only ones whose lives were at stake. Consider the people who hid the Jews and how they felt about allowing strangers into their homes.

Name _____   Date _____

Unit Outline:

The Upstairs Room

by Johanna Reiss

Day 1:
1. Assign a role to each group member:
   (a) *Secretary:* Someone to record the group assignments and discussions. In recording the discussions, the Secretary should describe the general discussion—who thought what—and then describe how the discussion ended. Was there a consensus?
   (b) *Taskmaster:* Someone to read instructions each day and keep the group on task.
   (c) *Assignment Collector:* Someone to collect assignments and turn them in each day.
   (d) *Librarian:* Someone to get the books and return them each day. The Librarian will also complete any research required.
   (e) *Activity Director:* Someone to organize group activities.
2. Identify group members who would like to read aloud.
3. Complete the Questionnaire sheet on your own. Upon completion, discuss your responses with your group. Why did you choose the items you did? Does your group have the same or differing opinions? Justify or defend your responses on the back of your paper.*
4. The Librarian needs to collect the books for group members.
5. The Taskmaster will read the introductory material aloud to the group so that all group members will have a good idea of what will be expected during the unit.
6. If there's still time left in the class period, begin reading the introduction aloud.

Day 2:
1. Read the introduction aloud. Discuss what new information about World War II your group learns. Why was this put at the beginning of this book?*
2. Read Chapter 1 aloud.
3. Fill out Day 2 Section Summary/Title. Make sure you read the directions carefully. This can be a group effort; however, each group member will be responsible for his/her own paper. This assignment will be turned in when you are finished reading the book.
4. This book has a lot of characters, and a character chart will help you to keep track of who is who. Begin making a chart of the important characters using your own paper. Include the following information:
   (a) name (you might include their relationship to the main character)
   (b) physical description (height, weight, hair color, eye color, etc.)
   (c) profession, hobbies, and interests
   (d) what they have lost or what has been taken away from them

   At the end of the unit, you will be turning in a final, polished copy, so you should work on a rough draft during the reading and rewrite your chart when you have completed the novel.

Day 3:
1. Read Chapter 2 aloud.
2. Fill out Section Summary/Title.

---

* All group discussions must be written up by the Secretary and turned in at the completion of the discussion.

Unit Outline: *The Upstairs Room*

      3. Add to character sheet if necessary.

      4. Group discussion: What is happening so far? How does Annie's life change because of the war? What would you do if you were in this situation? Why didn't Annie's mother want to go to America? Do you think the reason she gave was the real reason? Explain. How do you feel about Annie's father's treatment of her mother?*

Day 4:
      1. Read Chapter 3 aloud.

      2. Fill out Section Summary/Title worksheet.

      3. Add to your character sheet if necessary.

      4. Group Discussion: Did the de Leeuw family believe they would be safe in their new home outside of Winterswijk? Did you think they would be safe? Explain. Compare the attitudes of Annie's father and mother about the German occupation. Which one do you think had a better understanding of what was "really" happening? Explain.

      5. Librarians need to go to the library or check on a computer for information on Jewish traditions and information on what "kosher" means.

Day 5:
      1. Read Chapter 4. (At this point your group can decide if you want to continue reading aloud, or if you want to read silently.)

      2. Fill out Section Summary/Title worksheet.

      3. Work on character sheet.

      4. Librarian should present the information found on what kosher means to the Jews. Take notes as a group.*

Day 6:
      1. Read Chapter 5.

      2. Fill out Section Summary/Title worksheet.

      3. Add to character chart if necessary.

      4. On p. 71, Sini explains her milking diploma. If you were to receive a "diploma" like Sini, what would you receive your diploma in? On your own paper, make a diploma for yourself. (For example, I might make a diploma for house cleaning because it feels as if I do it all the time.) Next, brainstorm possible diplomas for five other people and explain why they should get those diplomas.

Day 7:
      1. Read Chapter 6.

      2. Fill out Section Summary/Title worksheet.

      3. Group discussion: Several people, at great personal risk, were willing to help Jews during the war: Reverend Zwaal, the Hanninks, the Oostervelds, for example. Explain why you think they would do this. Johann Oosterveld listened to what he called "the real news" on the radio. What did he mean by that? When might the "news" not be the news?*

---

* All group discussions must be written up by the Secretary and turned in at the completion of the discussion.

Unit Outline: *The Upstairs Room*

Day 8:
1. Read Chapter 7.
2. Fill out Section Summary/Title worksheet.
3. Imagine you are Annie or Sini, living with the Oostervelds during the war. Write a letter to "your" father. What would it say?

Day 9:
1. Read Chapter 8.
2. Fill out Section Summary/Title worksheet.
3. Add to your character chart if necessary.
4. Annie and Sini have hidden out in many different places. If our country were to be invaded right now, where would you go? Draw or explain the best, most secretive place you can think of to hide.

Day 10:
1. Read Chapter 9.
2. Fill out Section Summary/Title worksheet.
3. Annie and Sini made up rhymes during their stay with the Oostervelds. On p. 127 you can see the rhyme they made up for Opoe. Work with your group and create one of the unread rhymes for one of the other "family" members there. This can be a free verse rhyme, a limerick, or any other type of rhyme you know.

   On your own, create a fun, positive rhyme for a member of **your** family. Turn these in when you are finished.

Day 11:
1. Read Chapter 10.
2. Fill out Section Summary/Title worksheet.
3. Add to your character chart if necessary.
4. Complete Cause and Effect flowchart. The teacher will provide instructions. Turn in when finished.

Day 12:
1. Read Chapter 11.
2. Fill out Section Summary/Title worksheet.
3. Group discussion: When Johann went to hide out in Enchede, Dientje sent the girls back to the Hanninks. Why did she do this? How did Annie feel about this? How did you think Annie felt about the Oostervelds? Explain.*
4. As a group, complete the Importance Chart. You may use your Section Summary sheet or your observation list to help you.

Day 13:
1. Read Chapter 12 and Postscript.
2. Complete Section Summary/Title worksheet and turn in.
3. Complete character sheet. Final copy due tomorrow.
4. Begin working on the Holocaust Literature handout. The teacher will provide instructions. Use the Holocaust Essay Form for your final copy of the written assignment.

---

* All group discussions must be written up by the Secretary and turned in at the completion of the discussion.

Unit Outline: *The Upstairs Room*

Days 14–17: 1. The Taskmaster will read the instructions from the project/
presentation sheet. The group should formulate some ideas, with
the Secretary taking notes. During these days, your group should
be putting together your presentation and related assignment, as well as rehearsing for
the class presentation.

Determine who will be responsible for what parts. Before you present, you will need to
turn in a paper neatly written in ink with all of your names in the heading that will
outline the responsibilities for each group member. Each member will be graded individually for his/her part in the presentation.*

Days 18–20: Class presentations. There will be a five-question quiz at the end of each presentation.

_____

* All group discussions must be written up by the Secretary and turned in at the completion of the discussion.

The Upstairs Room
by Johanna Reiss
Day 1: Questionnaire

Read the following questions and determine for yourself the answers you think fit best. You may choose two or three items per question.

1. *What words best describe **prejudice**?*

   _____ obstinate   _____ single-minded   _____ biased

   _____ forceful   _____ conceited   _____ ignorant

   _____ stubborn   _____ poor   _____ wealthy

   _____ judgmental   _____ unloved   _____ opinionated

2. *What do you think causes a person to become prejudiced?*

   _____ He/She was just born that way.

   _____ His/Her parents taught him/her to be that way by their example.

   _____ He/She observes incidents on television and at school.

   _____ He/She lives in an area where he/she is in the minority.

   _____ He/She lives in an area where he/she is in the vast majority.

   _____ He/She has been the victim in a race-related incident.

   _____ He/She has been the victim in an ethnic-related incident.

   _____ His/Her religion teaches supremacy of one race over another.

3. *How would you recognize a prejudiced person?*

   _____ From the way he/she lives.

   _____ From his/her facial expressions.

   _____ From his/her actions toward athletes, comedians, or politicians of different ethnic, racial, or religious backgrounds.

   _____ From the way he/she teases, taunts people.

4. *How would you cure a prejudiced person?*

   _____ With love and kindness, understanding.

   _____ With reasoning and knowledge.

   _____ By giving him/her a taste of his/her own medicine.

   _____ By getting someone to beat or frighten him/her.

   _____ There is no cure.

Name _____ Date _____

The Upstairs Room
Summaries and Titles

Directions:

1. Each member of the group will keep track of each of the section summaries in the book and turn in this assignment at the end of the reading. **Each of you will also be responsible for predicting future events based on what you have just read.**

2. After reading each day, look back over the pages read and think about what you might title the reading for that day if you were the author of the book. After the group members have individually decided on chapter titles, have a group discussion on why the titles were given. Which title does the group agree is the most accurate?

	Section Summary and Prediction	**Section Title**
Day 2 Pages read:		Why?
Day 3 Pages read:		Why?
Day 4 Pages read:		Why?
Day 5 Pages read:		Why?

(continued)

Holocaust Literature:
Study Guides to 12 Stories of Courage

Name _____ Date _____

The Upstairs Room
Summaries and Titles *(continued)*

	Section Summary and Prediction	**Section Title**
Day 6 Pages read:		Why?
Day 7 Pages read:		Why?
Day 8 Pages read:		Why?
Day 9 Pages read:		Why?
Day 10 Pages read:		Why?

(continued)

Holocaust Literature:
Study Guides to 12 Stories of Courage

The Upstairs Room
Summaries and Titles *(continued)*

	Section Summary and Prediction	Section Title
Day 11 Pages read:		Why?
Day 12 Pages read:		Why?

The Upstairs Room
Day 11: Cause and Effect

Show how the events in a novel determine future events by filling in the squares with causes and effects from *The Upstairs Room.* Begin each sentence with *Since* or *Because.* When you begin a sentence with either of these two words, you create a complex sentence, and there needs to be a comma at the end of the first clause. The first one has been done for you.

Because Annie's mother did not want to escape to America, the de Leeuw family was in Holland when the Nazis invaded.

Since the de Leeuw family was in Holland when the Nazis invaded,

Holocaust Literature:
Study Guides to 12 Stories of Courage

Name _____   Date _____

The Upstairs Room
Day 12: Importance Chart

On the lines below, list the 10 events (in order of occurrence) that your group considers the most important events in the book. Then explain why.

1. _____ ,

   because _____ .

2. _____ ,

   because _____ .

3. _____ ,

   because _____ .

4. _____ ,

   because _____ .

5. _____ ,

   because _____ .

6. _____ ,

   because _____ .

7. _____ ,

   because _____ .

8. _____ ,

   because _____ .

9. _____ ,

   because _____ .

10. _____ ,

   because _____ .

Name _____ Date _____

The Upstairs Room
Grading Sheet

Assignment	Possible Points	Student ✓	Teacher ✓	Points
1. Questionnaire Responses				
2. Day 2: Group Discussion				
3. Day 3: Group Discussion				
4. Day 4: Group Discussion				
5. Day 5: Notes on Kosher				
6. Day 6: Diplomas				
7. Day 7: Group Discussion				
8. Day 8: Letter to Father				
9. Day 9: Hiding Place				
10. Day 10: Rhymes				
11. Day 11: Cause and Effect				
12. Day 12: Group Discussion				
13. Day 12: Importance Chart				
14. Section Summaries/Titles				
15. Character Chart				
16. Day 13: Holocaust Literature				
17. Day 13: Holocaust Essay				
18. Character Bag				
19. Class Presentation				
20. Class Quizzes				
21. Group Participation				
			Total Pts.	
			Grade	

Holocaust Literature:
Study Guides to 12 Stories of Courage

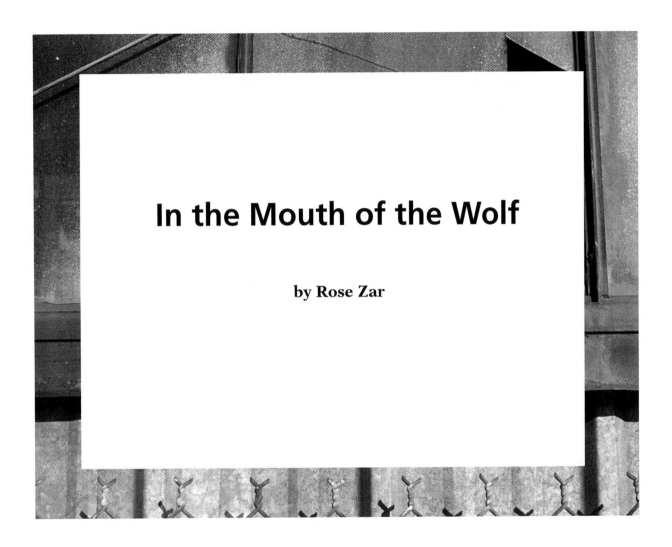

In the Mouth of the Wolf

by Rose Zar

In the Mouth of the Wolf

by Rose Zar

To the Student

This is not a concentration camp story. The action of this story takes place in Poland, one of the first countries that Germany took over during World War II. Ruszka was a Jewish girl whose parents decided that she would have a better chance of surviving the German tyranny if she were on her own. The interesting thing about this story is that her parents were absolutely right—not only on this issue, but also in teaching her some other very valuable lessons that helped her survive. Her parents must have been very smart, and you'll be impressed with Ruszka's quick intelligence as you read how she got out of some pretty sticky situations and survived to tell about them.

When you read this story, think about how *you* would have reacted to the situations Ruszka faced. Would you have been able to bluff your way out? Also notice that Ruszka was well educated, and that it was her knowledge of the Polish language and her study of Catholicism that saved her. She lived falsely as a Roman Catholic from 1939 to 1945 in order to survive. And as the title of the story indicates, Ruszka lived "in the mouth of" danger because she managed to work as a nanny for an important SS officer.

Be sure to emphasize these ideas to the class when you give your presentation. It might also help to have a map available, because Ruszka did so much moving around. It might be confusing to the class if you call her by her false name—Wanda—so be sure to clarify the name situation.

Unit Outline:

In the Mouth of the Wolf

by Rose Zar

Day 1:

1. Assign a role to each group member:

    (a) *Secretary:* Someone to record the group assignments and discussions. In recording the discussions, the Secretary should describe the general discussion—who thought what—and then describe how the discussion ended. Was there a consensus?

    (b) *Taskmaster:* Someone to read instructions each day and keep the group on task.

    (c) *Assignment Collector:* Someone to make sure all assignments get turned in each day.

    (d) *Librarian:* Someone to get the books and return them each day. The Librarian will also complete any research required.

    (e) *Activity Director:* Someone to organize group activities.

2. Identify group members who would like to read aloud.

3. Complete the Questionnaire sheet on your own. Upon completion, discuss your responses with your group. Why did you choose the items you did? Does your group have the same or differing opinions? Justify or defend your responses on the back of your paper.*

4. The Librarian needs to get the books at this point.

5. The Taskmaster will read the introductory material aloud to the group so that all group members will have a good idea of what will be expected during the unit.

6. If there's still time left in the class period, begin reading aloud.

Day 2:

1. Read aloud the prologue and from the first chapter, "Escape from the Ghetto," to the break on p. 19.

2. Fill out Day 2 Section Summary/Title worksheet. This can be a group effort; however, each group member will be responsible for his/her own paper. This assignment will be turned in when you're finished reading the book.

3. Start a chart of the advice that the author gets from various sources, but especially from her father.* Turn this in when you're finished reading the book.

Day 3:

1. Finish reading the first chapter and to the break on p. 34 in Chapter 2, "The Shop in Rudniki."

2. Fill out Section Summary/Title worksheet for these pages.

3. Continue working on the advice chart. Each of you needs to begin thinking of the advice *you* have gotten from various people, but especially from your parents. An assignment will come later. Discuss this idea as a group to help each other remember.

---

* All group discussions must be written up by the Secretary and turned in at the completion of the discussion.

Unit Outline: *In the Mouth of the Wolf*

4. Group activity: Make a chart* that you will later make into a poster to show the class at the end of this unit. This chart will illustrate World War II survival skills as learned from Rose Zar. For example, one of the first survival skills she learned is to travel alone. What are some others? This chart will be presented to the class when you do your book presentation.

Day 4:
1. Finish reading the second chapter, "The Shop in Rudniki."
2. Fill out Section Summary/Title worksheet, advice chart, and survival skills chart.
3. Spend a couple of minutes sharing with your group some specific pieces of advice you have received from your father or some other family member. Begin writing a paper today and finish it tomorrow in class on the topic of family advice. In this paper discuss what advice you have gotten and how the advice was or was not helpful.

Day 5:
1. Read Chapter 3, "The Man in the Railway Cap" and Chapter 4, "The Bunker" to the break on p. 67.
2. Fill out Section Summary/Title worksheet, advice chart, and survival skills chart.
3. Finish yesterday's assignment and turn it in today. If you don't get it done, take it home tonight and turn it in tomorrow.

Day 6:
1. Read to the end of "The Bunker."
2. Fill out Section Summary/Title worksheet, advice chart, and survival skills chart.
3. Do the Copy Change assignment. Continue working on it tomorrow, and have it ready to turn in the day after tomorrow.

Day 7:
1. Read "Christmas Eve" and "Friends and Enemies."
2. Fill out Section Summary/Title worksheet, advice chart, and survival skills chart.
3. Finish the Copy Change assignment and turn it in. If you don't finish, take it home tonight and have it ready to turn in when you come to class tomorrow.

Day 8:
1. Read "Potatoes for the SS" and "A Summer Interlude" to the break on p. 128.
2. Fill out Section Summary/Title worksheet, advice chart, and survival skills chart.
3. Do the Figurative Language worksheet. Due today.

Day 9:
1. Read the rest of "A Summer Interlude" and to the end of "The Kommandant."
2. Fill out Section Summary/Title worksheet, advice chart, and survival skills chart.
3. Do Colon worksheet. When you're finished, ask the teacher for the answer sheet so you can correct your work. Then answer the question at the bottom of the worksheet and turn in your assignment.

Day 10:
1. Read "Gestapo on My Trail" and to the break of "Scenes from the Hurricane's Eye" on p. 164.
2. Fill out Section Summary/Title worksheet, advice chart, and survival skills chart.

---

* All group discussions must be written up by the Secretary and turned in at the completion of the discussion.

Unit Outline: *In the Mouth of the Wolf*

Day 11:   1. Read the rest of "Scenes from the Hurricane's Eye" to the break on p. 184.

2. Fill out Section Summary/Title worksheet, advice chart, and survival skills chart.

3. Do the Cause and Effect flowchart.

Day 12:   1. Read the rest of "The End in Sight" and to the break on p. 203.

2. Fill out Section Summary/Title worksheet, advice chart, and survival skills chart.

3. Group discussion of the Importance Chart. Turn one in for the group.*

Day 13:   1. Read to the end of the book.

2. Fill in the last Section Summary/Title worksheet, advice chart*, and survival skills chart* and turn them in.

3. Begin working on the Holocaust Literature handout. The teacher will provide instructions. Use the Holocaust Essay Form for your final copy of the written assignment.

Days 14–17:   1. Holocaust essay due.

2. Begin planning the presentation that will be given to the class. The Taskmaster will read the instructions from the Class Presentation sheet. The group should formulate some ideas, with the Secretary taking notes. During the next four days, your group should be putting together your presentation and related assignments, as well as rehearsing for the class presentation.

Determine who will be responsible for what parts. Before you present, you will need to turn in a paper neatly written in ink with all of your names in the heading that will outline the responsibilities for each group member. Each member will be graded individually for his/her part in the presentation.*

Days 18–20:   Class presentations. There will be a five-question quiz at the end of each presentation.

---

* All group discussions must be written up by the Secretary and turned in at the completion of the discussion.

Name _____   Date _____

In the Mouth of the Wolf

by Rose Zar
Day 1: Questionnaire

Read the following questions and determine for yourself the answers you think are best. You may choose two or three items from each group.

1. *What words best describe **prejudice**?*

   _____ obstinate   _____ single-minded   _____ biased

   _____ forceful   _____ conceited   _____ ignorant

   _____ stubborn   _____ poor   _____ wealthy

   _____ judgmental   _____ unloved   _____ opinionated

2. *What do you think causes a person to become prejudiced?*

   _____ He/She was just born that way.

   _____ His/Her parents taught him/her to be that way by their example.

   _____ He/She observes incidents on television and at school.

   _____ He/She lives in an area where he/she is in the minority.

   _____ He/She lives in an area where he/she is in the vast majority.

   _____ He/She has been the victim in a race-related incident.

   _____ He/She has been the victim in an ethnic-related incident.

   _____ His/Her religion teaches supremacy of one race over another.

3. *How would you recognize a prejudiced person?*

   _____ From the way he/she lives.

   _____ From his/her facial expressions.

   _____ From his/her actions toward athletes, comedians, or politicians of
           different ethnic, racial, or religious backgrounds.

   _____ From the way he/she teases, taunts people.

4. *How would you cure a prejudiced person?*

   _____ With love and kindness, understanding.

   _____ With reasoning and knowledge.

   _____ By giving him/her a taste of his/her own medicine.

   _____ By getting someone to beat or frighten him/her.

   _____ There is no cure.

Holocaust Literature:
Study Guides to 12 Stories of Courage

Name _____ Date _____

In the Mouth of the Wolf
Summaries and Titles

Directions:

1. Each member of the group will keep track of each of the section summaries in the book and turn in this assignment at the end of the reading. **Each of you will also be responsible for predicting future events based on what you have just read.**

2. After reading each day, look back over the pages read and think about what you might title the reading for that day if you were the author of the book. After the group members have individually decided on chapter titles, have a group discussion on why the titles were given. Which title does the group agree is the most accurate?

	Section Summary and Prediction	Section Title
Day 2 Pages read:		Why?
Day 3 Pages read:		Why?
Day 4 Pages read:		Why?
Day 5 Pages read:		Why?

(continued)

Holocaust Literature:
Study Guides to 12 Stories of Courage

In the Mouth of the Wolf
Summaries and Titles *(continued)*

	Section Summary and Prediction	Section Title
Day 6 Pages read:		Why?
Day 7 Pages read:		Why?
Day 8 Pages read:		Why?
Day 9 Pages read:		Why?
Day 10 Pages read:		Why?

(continued)

In the Mouth of the Wolf
Summaries and Titles *(continued)*

	Section Summary and Prediction	**Section Title**
Day 11 Pages read:		Why?
Day 12 Pages read:		Why?
Day 13 Pages read:		Why?

Holocaust Literature:
Study Guides to 12 Stories of Courage

In the Mouth of the Wolf
Day 6: Copy Change Assignment

This is the description found in the prologue.

Night. The coming dawn is a knife edge on the eastern horizon as the train rolls south through the forests and fields of central Poland. The train's lights are out, for this is wartime. Behind the blacked-out windows of the third-class passenger cars—the only ones available for civilian travel now that the Germans occupy the country—every inch of space is packed with people and baggage. The darkened carriages vibrate with a restless hum. A hungry infant cries and is quickly stilled. From a compartment come the sounds of laughter and lively conversation. In the corridor a man deals cards. Another passes around a bottle. Some sleep on rolled-up coats or bundles. Others try to. And some, like the young woman in the gray coat with the fur collar, simply sit staring into the darkness, awaiting whatever challenge the new day will bring.

The young woman's name is Ruszka Guterman. She is nineteen years old and already that night, she has looked on the face of death twice. But no trace of fear marks her face nor any hint of the gnawing anguish she feels inside. The people on the train do not even suspect she is Jewish. But I know, just as I also know what she is feeling in her heart on that long night ride south. I know . . . because I was there.

I was that young woman.

Assignment

In your mind, picture an unforgettable scene. For me it was when I was in kindergarten, and our family had just been in a car accident. When you describe this scene, tell it in the present tense, as if describing a photograph, because the scene you choose will actually be an indelible photograph in your mind. Notice how dramatic the scene becomes when you use the present tense.

Night. The oncoming car ignores the red light and plows on through the intersection and into the side of another car. There is a disturbing silence after the collision. No screaming. No yelling. Nothing. The driver of the hit car is unharmed, as are two passengers in the back seat. The mother, a passenger in the front seat, however, is unconscious, slumped over. Her head has smashed into the windshield. In her arms she holds a toddler who seems somewhat alert, although blood trickles from a cut on her forehead. Still, there are no voices, no sounds in the eerie night air. Slowly, the scene comes alive. A small girl in the back seat is carried out, but when they try to set her down, she screams. She can't walk. An older girl in the middle of the front seat looks up, is surprised to see the windshield crumbled, and wonders what she's doing on the floor of the car. Suddenly a sticky liquid pours into her eyes, and she

(continued)

Holocaust Literature:
Study Guides to 12 Stories of Courage

In the Mouth of the Wolf
Day 6: Copy Change Assignment (continued)

temporarily loses sight. Later on, she will learn that her face bounced off the dashboard several times before she blacked out. Now the screams of the ambulance can be heard in the distance. I know just what she is feeling in her on that warm summer night. I know . . . because I was there.

I was that older girl.

See what ideas you can get from the paragraph that Rose Zar wrote. Your paragraph, like mine, probably will not follow the pattern exactly, but that's okay. The idea is to capture as much of the smells, the sights, the sounds, the feeling of the scene as you remember it.

119

In the Mouth of the Wolf
Day 8: Figurative Language

Rose Zar's writing throughout this book is vivid with imagery. She makes ample use of literary devices. Read the definitions of these kinds of devices and then identify each quotation below with the correct label.

Simile: A comparison between unlike things using the words *like* or *as*.
               Example: Tears flowed like wine.

Irony: Expression in which the intended meaning of the words is the opposite of their usual sense, or an event or result that is the opposite of what is expected.

Metaphor: Showing a comparison between two things, and treating the one as if it *were* the other. Similar to a simile, only there's no clue word, *like* or *as*.
               Example: The inspector was a great bear of a man.

_____   1. . . . where the turmoil of daily events was as inconsequential as an afternoon sun shower. (p. 28)

_____   2. That night, all over Poland, there were Jews like me, desperately seeking shelter. But the inn was full. The well of human kindness was empty. Every door was slammed in our faces. And all the while, the church bells rang. (p. 90)

_____   3. I walked through a world of enemies with a deadly sword hanging over my head. (p. 122)

_____   4. He spoke with the soothing purr of a cat who has just come across a fledgling. (p. 131)

_____   5. I was living in the wolf's mouth now, and, believe me, there is no better refuge in the world. (p. 159)

_____   6. Then, still staring out the window, the officer began firing questions at me in rapid order like a drill sergeant shaking down a squad of recruits. (p. 138)

_____   7. I could never forget that my life hung suspended by a very slender thread. A glittering sword, posed to cut it off, was never far away. (p. 184)

_____   8. He was extremely handsome, but his eyes had a cold, ruthless glitter like those of a bird of prey. (p. 138)

In the Mouth of the Wolf
Day 9: Colons

A colon is a punctuation mark that is used before a long quotation, an explanation, an example, or a series. It is also used as a stylistic tool to focus the reader's attention on what is to come. It's kind of like a *ta da!*

The following sentences were taken from this book, but the colons have been replaced by commas. Insert the colons where you think they belong. Then check your work by looking up the original sentences in the book.

1. Of the whole Polish population, delinquents like these were absolutely the worst, thoroughly vicious and completely without pity.

2. To pass as a Polish girl I had to talk like one, quick and vulgar, saying things that two weeks ago would have made me blush.

3. Most of the passenger cars were reserved for Germans, military personnel, civilians, and *Volksdeutsche* (ethnic Germans).

4. She was knitting a glove, a five-fingered glove, not a mitten.

5. The bunker was designed and provisioned to accommodate twelve people, my parents, my little sister, and my aunt; Mr. Banasz; Mr. Israelevitch, his wife, and two daughters; and Mr. and Mrs. Blaustein and their daughter.

6. He was my father again, tough, decisive, firmly in command.

7. That was what our friendship meant to me, a reminder of who I really was.

8. She was a lovely person, intelligent, kind, attractive in her own way, and extremely gentle.

9. We learned all about babies, how to diaper them; how to hold them; how to feed and burp them.

10. I had other papers in my drawer as well, my medical insurance book, a few photos of myself for official documents, and a picture of Mr. and Mrs. Banasz and their dog.

In the Mouth of the Wolf
Day 11: Cause and Effect

Show how events in a story determine future events by filling in the squares with causes and effects from *In the Mouth of the Wolf*. Begin each sentence with *Since* or *Because*. When you begin a sentence with either of these two words, you create a complex sentence, and there needs to be a comma at the end of the first clause. The first one has been done for you.

Because the Germans have invaded Poland, Rose's family decides that Rose will have a better chance to survive if she goes off on her own.

Since she is on her own, Rose . . .

Holocaust Literature:
Study Guides to 12 Stories of Courage

Name _____ Date _____

In the Mouth of the Wolf
Day 12: Importance Chart

On the lines below, list the 10 events (in order of occurrence) that your group considers the most important events in the book. Then explain why.

1. _____,
   because _____.

2. _____,
   because _____.

3. _____,
   because _____.

4. _____,
   because _____.

5. _____,
   because _____.

6. _____,
   because _____.

7. _____,
   because _____.

8. _____,
   because _____.

9. _____,
   because _____.

10. _____,
    because _____.

Name _____   Date _____

In the Mouth of the Wolf
Grading Sheet

Assignment	Possible Points	Student ✓	Teacher ✓	Points
1. Questionnaire Responses				
2. Day 4: Advice Paper				
3. Day 6: Copy Change				
4. Day 8: Figurative Language				
5. Day 9: Colons				
6. Day 11: Cause and Effect				
7. Day 12: Importance Chart				
8. Section Summaries/Titles				
9. Advice Chart				
10. Survival Skills Chart				
11. Day 13: Holocaust Literature				
12. Day 13: Holocaust Essay				
13. Character Bag				
14. Class Presentation				
15. Class Quizzes				
16. Group Participation				
			Total Pts.	
			Grade	

Farewell to Manzanar

by Jeanne Wakatsuki Houston
and
James D. Houston

Name _____ Date _____

Farewell to Manzanar

by Jeanne Wakatsuki Houston
and James Houston

To the Student

When we hear about World War II, we generally think of the war in Europe. Although the conflicts in Europe were a major part of the war, we often forget about the conflict with Japan. On December 7, 1941, the Japanese initiated a surprise attack on Pearl Harbor, Hawaii causing America to go to war against Japan. Following this order, President Roosevelt gave the war department permission to detain anyone who might be a threat. This included all Japanese-Americans.

In 1942, all Japanese-Americans living on the west coast of the United States were sent to internment camps: camps enclosed with barbed wire and guarded by gun-wielding military men. Jeanne Wakatsuki Houston was one of these Japanese-Americans who, along with her family, was sent to one of these Americanized concentration camps.

Although these camps did not have gas chambers or ovens, the prisoners were forced to work and to give up most of their family traditions. They were fed Americanized Japanese food which didn't digest well. The living quarters were about the size of a walk-in closet, but made to hold 10 to 12 people. Like the European Jews, the Japanese could not understand why they were forced to live like prisoners.

As you prepare for your presentation, consider the reasons for the internment of the Japanese. You might explain to the class America's rationalization for this. Also consider the breakdown of family values inside the camp. Compare this to the breakdown of the Jewish family values in Europe during the war. You might also compare America's treatment of the Japanese to the Nazis' treatment of the Jews at this time.

Name _____   Date _____

Unit Outline:

Farewell to Manzanar

by Jeanne Wakatsuki Houston
and James Houston

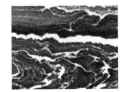

Day 1:   1. Assign a role to each group member:

(a) *Secretary:* Someone to record the group assignments and discussions. In recording the discussions, the Secretary should describe the general discussion—who thought what—and then describe how the discussion ended. Was there a consensus?

(b) *Taskmaster:* Someone to read instructions each day and keep the group on task.

(c) *Assignment Collector:* Someone to collect assignments and turn them in each day.

(d) *Librarian:* Someone to get the books and return them each day. The Librarian will also complete any research required.

(e) *Activity Director:* Someone to organize group activities.

2. Identify group members who would like to read aloud.

3. Complete the Questionnaire sheet on your own. Upon completion, discuss your responses with your group. Why did you choose the items you did? Does your group have the same or differing opinions? Justify or defend your responses.*

4. The Librarian needs to collect the books for group members.

5. The Taskmaster will read the introductory material aloud to the group so that all group members will have a good idea of what will be expected during the unit.

6. Read pp. *ix–xiii.* The chronology and terms used in this book will help you to better understand the content.

Day 2:   1. Read Chapter 1 aloud.

2. Fill out Day 2 Section Summary/Title sheet. Make sure you read the directions carefully. This can be a group effort; however, each group member will be responsible for his/her own paper. This assignment will be turned in when you are finished reading the book.

3. This book has a lot of characters, and a character chart will help you to keep track of who is who. Begin by making a chart of the important characters using your own paper. Include the following information:

(a) name (you might include their relationship to the main character)

(b) physical description (height, weight, hair color, eye color, etc.)

(c) profession, hobbies, and interests

(d) what they have lost or what has been taken away from them

At the end of the unit you will be turning in a final, polished copy, so you should work on a rough draft during the reading and rewrite your chart when you have completed the novel.

---

* All group discussions must be written up by the Secretary and turned in at the completion of the discussion.

Holocaust Literature:
Study Guides to 12 Stories of Courage

Name _____   Date _____

Unit Outline: *Farewell to Manzanar*

Day 3:
1. Read Chapters 2, 3, and 4. (At this point your group can determine whether you will read aloud or silently.)
2. Fill out Section Summary/Title worksheet.
3. Add to your character sheet if necessary.
4. Copy Change assignment.

Day 4:
1. Read Chapters 5, 6, and 7.
2. Fill out Section Summary/Title worksheet.
3. Add to your character sheet if necessary.
4. Group discussion: In your group, discuss the following questions:*
   (a) What types of people suffered the most during World War II? Why were they made to suffer?
   (b) What did Jeanne's father mean when he told the guard, "When your mother and father are fighting, do you want them to kill each other or do you just want them to stop fighting?"
5. In Chapter 6, Jeanne wrote about her father. From reading this chapter you can tell that she admired him tremendously but was a little frightened of him. Think of a person like that in your life. It may be a male or a female. Maybe this person is a parent, or maybe a grandparent, friend of the family, or even a teacher. Write a one-page paper describing this person in the same manner Jeanne described her father in Chapter 6. Remember that the final copy you turn in should be in ink.
6. Librarians need to go to the library or check on the computer for a map of California. Bring a copy with you to class tomorrow.

Day 5:
1. Read Chapters 8 and 9.
2. Complete Section Summary/Title worksheet.
3. Add to your character sheet if necessary.
4. Group discussion: Librarians need to present the map of California. Based on the information Jeanne has given you, try to locate the different places the Wakatsuki family has been to. Now locate Japan in relation to these places. Do you think the Japanese in the United States—California in particular—were a threat to the United States? Specifically, why did we Americans intern the Japanese? Do you think it was right?*

Day 6:
1. Read Chapters 10 and 11.
2. Complete Section Summary/Title worksheet.
3. Add to your character sheet if necessary.
4. Group discussion: Jeanne maintains that the style of living at Manzanar caused her family to break down. Brainstorm some traditions her family lost when they were sent to Manzanar. Now brainstorm traditions your family has that you would not want to lose (for example, family camping trips, Christmas traditions, etc.).*

---

* All group discussions must be written up by the Secretary and turned in at the completion of the discussion.

128   *Holocaust Literature:*
Study Guides to 12 Stories of Courage

Unit Outline: *Farewell to Manzanar*

Day 7:
1. Read Chapters 12 and 13.
2. Complete Section Summary/Title worksheet.
3. Group discussion: Have your Librarian look up "irony." Discuss how irony relates to Manzanar and the families' attempts to create normalcy in this Americanized "concentration camp." Look also at the irony of the loyal Japanese-Americans in these camps. Write down specific examples from the book of this type of irony and explain why your group considers these examples to be ironic situations.

Day 8:
1. Read Chapters 14 and 15.
2. Complete Section Summary/Title worksheet.
3. Add to your character sheet if necessary.
4. Group discussion: One reason the Japanese were interned was the hysteria caused by the bombing of Pearl Harbor. The American government became fearful that all people of Japanese ancestry could be spies. That was over 50 years ago. How have attitudes toward Japanese-Americans changed?

   In your group, discuss what people tend to be discriminated against in America today. Also, what types of people are discriminated against in your hometown? at your school? Explain the possible reasons for this discrimination.*

Day 9:
1. Read Chapters 16, 17, and 18.
2. Complete Section Summary/Title worksheet.
3. Add to your character sheet if necessary.

Day 10:
1. Read Chapters 19 and 20.
2. Complete Section Summary/Title worksheet.
3. Add to your character sheet if necessary.
4. During the time Jeanne was interned, the president of the United States was Franklin Delano Roosevelt (known as FDR). Write a letter to President Roosevelt explaining the problems of the internment camps, what the conditions are, and whether interning the Japanese is a good thing or a mistake. This should be a formal, persuasive letter, at least one page in length. Due at the end of Day 12.

Day 11:
1. Read Chapter 21.
2. Complete Section Summary/Title worksheet.
3. Add to your character sheet if necessary.
4. Complete Cause and Effect flowchart. The teacher will provide instructions. Turn in when finished.

Day 12:
1. Read Chapter 22.
2. Complete Section Summary/Title worksheet.
3. Complete final copy of character chart.

---

* All group discussions must be written up by the Secretary and turned in at the completion of the discussion.

Unit Outline: *Farewell to Manzanar*

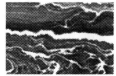

    4. As a group, complete the Importance Chart. You may use your section summary sheet or your observation list to help you.

Day 13:   1. Begin working on Holocaust Literature handout. The teacher will provide instructions. Use the Holocaust Essay Form for your final copy of the written assignment.

    2. Work on any unfinished assignments.

    3. Turn in character chart and Section Summary/Title worksheet. Make sure they are complete, with your name at the top.

Days 14–17:   The Taskmaster will read the instructions from the Class Presentation sheet. The group should formulate some ideas, with the Secretary taking notes. During these days, your group should be putting together your presentation and related assignments, as well as rehearsing for the class presentation.

Determine who will be responsible for what parts. Before you present, you will need to turn in a paper neatly written in ink with all of your names in the heading that will outline the responsibilities for each group member. Each member will be graded individually on his/her part in the presentation.*

Days 18–20:   Class presentations. There will be a five-question quiz at the end of each presentation.

---

* All group discussions must be written up by the Secretary and turned in at the completion of the discussion.

Name _____ Date _____

Farewell to Manzanar

by Jeanne Wakatsuki Houston and James D. Houston
Day 1: Questionnaire

Read the following questions and determine for yourself the answers you think fit best. You may choose two or three items per question.

1. *What words best describe* **prejudice**?

   _____ obstinate   _____ single-minded   _____ biased

   _____ forceful   _____ conceited   _____ ignorant

   _____ stubborn   _____ poor   _____ wealthy

   _____ judgmental   _____ unloved   _____ opinionated

2. *What do you think causes a person to become prejudiced?*

   _____ He/She was just born that way.

   _____ His/Her parents taught him/her to be that way by their example.

   _____ He/She observes incidents on television and at school.

   _____ He/She lives in an area where he/she is in the minority.

   _____ He/She lives in an area where he/she is in the vast majority.

   _____ He/She has been the victim in a race-related incident.

   _____ He/She has been the victim in an ethnic-related incident.

   _____ His/Her religion teaches supremacy of one race over another.

3. *How would you recognize a prejudiced person?*

   _____ From the way he/she lives.

   _____ From his/her facial expressions.

   _____ From his/her actions toward athletes, comedians, or politicians of different ethnic, racial, or religious backgrounds.

   _____ From the way he/she teases, taunts people.

4. *How would you cure a prejudiced person?*

   _____ With love and kindness, understanding.

   _____ With reasoning and knowledge.

   _____ By giving him/her a taste of his/her own medicine.

   _____ By getting someone to beat or frighten him/her.

   _____ There is no cure.

Holocaust Literature:
Study Guides to 12 Stories of Courage

Farewell to Manzanar
Summaries and Titles

Directions:

1. Each member of the group will keep track of each of the section summaries in the book and turn in this assignment at the end of the reading. **Each of you will also be responsible for predicting future events based on what you have just read.**

2. After reading each day, look back over the pages read and think about what you might title the reading for that day if you were the author of the book. After the group members have individually decided on chapter titles, have a group discussion on why the titles were given. Which title does the group agree is the most accurate?

	Section Summary and Prediction	Section Title
Day 2 Pages read:		Why?
Day 3 Pages read:		Why?
Day 4 Pages read:		Why?
Day 5 Pages read:		Why?

(continued)

Farewell to Manzanar
Summaries and Titles *(continued)*

	Section Summary and Prediction	**Section Title**
Day 6 Pages read:		Why?
Day 7 Pages read:		Why?
Day 8 Pages read:		Why?
Day 9 Pages read:		Why?
Day 10 Pages read:		Why?

(continued)

Farewell to Manzanar
Summaries and Titles *(continued)*

	Section Summary and Prediction	**Section Title**
Day 11 Pages read:		Why?
Day 12 Pages read:		Why?

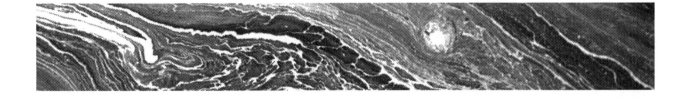

Holocaust Literature:
Study Guides to 12 Stories of Courage

Farewell to Manzanar
Day 3: Copy Change Assignment

This paragraph is found on p. 42:

That's how I remember him before he disappeared. He was not a great man. He was a poser, a braggart, and a tyrant. But he had held onto his self-respect, he dreamed grand dreams, and he could work well at any talk he turned his hand to: he could raise vegetables, sail a boat, plead a case in small claims court, sing Japanese poems, make false teeth, carve a pig. Whatever he did had flourished.

Assignment

In your mind, picture someone who is very important to you: someone you look up to and admire. Think about what this person does that makes him or her special. With that person in mind, you are going to copy the format of Wakatsuki's writing, but change the words so that it fits your special person. You will turn in a final copy in ink for a grade.

For me, a special person would be my father. He has always been there for me, making sure I stayed on the right track and achieved the most I could. He rarely lost his temper with me, and when he did he would sit me down and explain why. My father is a very special person. Here's my copy change:

That's how I will always remember him. He was not a self-conscious man. He could have been far more controlling than he was. He was demanding, a money miser, and had high expectations. But he could also be understanding, he held his anger, and he could talk us into doing anything he wanted: plant his garden without realizing it was work, get up early to paint the house, take piano lessons, realize dreams could become reality, go to college. Whatever he did, he did out of love.

If you need help with this assignment, refer to the paragraph from the book and to the paragraph I wrote to see what kind of information you will need. You really have quite a bit of freedom to change the words to describe the scene as you remember it. Good luck!

Farewell to Manzanar
Day 11: Cause and Effect

Show how events in a story determine future events by filling in the squares with causes and effects from *Farewell to Manzanar*. Begin each sentence with *Since* or *Because*. When you begin a sentence with either of these two words, you create a complex sentence, and there needs to be a comma at the end of the first clause. The first one has been done for you.

Because Jeanne Wakatsuki was Japanese, her family was forced to move to an internment camp in California.

Since the Wakatsuki family was forced to move to an internment camp,

Holocaust Literature:
Study Guides to 12 Stories of Courage

Name _____ Date _____

Farewell to Manzanar
Day 12: Importance Chart

On the lines below, list the 10 events (in order of occurrence) that your group considers the most important events in the book. Then explain why.

1. _____ ,

   because _____ .

2. _____ ,

   because _____ .

3. _____ ,

   because _____ .

4. _____ ,

   because _____ .

5. _____ ,

   because _____ .

6. _____ ,

   because _____ .

7. _____ ,

   because _____ .

8. _____ ,

   because _____ .

9. _____ ,

   because _____ .

10. _____ ,

   because _____ .

Holocaust Literature:
Study Guides to 12 Stories of Courage

Name _____   Date _____

Farewell to Manzanar
Grading Sheet

Assignment	Possible Points	Student ✓	Teacher ✓	Points
1. Questionnaire Responses				
2. Day 3: Copy Change				
3. Day 4: Group Discussion				
4. Day 4: Description Essay				
5. Day 5: Group Discussion				
6. Day 6: Group Discussion				
7. Day 7: Group Discussion				
8. Day 8: Group Discussion				
9. Day 10: Letter to the President				
10. Day 11: Cause and Effect				
11. Day 12: Importance Chart				
12. Day 13: Holocaust Literature				
13. Day 13: Holocaust Essay				
14. Section Summary/Title				
15. Character Chart				
16. Character Bag				
17. Class Presentation				
18. Class Quizzes				
19. Group Participation				
			Total Pts.	
			Grade	

Kindertransport

by Olga Levy Drucker

Kindertransport

by Olga Levy Drucker

To the Student

Kindertransport is **not** a story about Nazi atrocities. It is also not a book about battles or daring escapes. It **is** a story about the heroism exhibited throughout Europe by ordinary people during World War II. This book shows how common it was for people to do uncommon things.

Jews were slowly becoming aware that their children would be killed in the concentration camps, so a *kindertransport* was set up to get Jewish children out of occupied areas as quickly as possible. Children were evacuated by cars, trains, boats—all forms of transportation. Olga was sent to England with other children, where she stayed with several different families until the war was over.

At the beginning of the story you will notice that the person telling the story sounds like a child—and Olga *was* a child then. Keep that in mind when you follow her to England. Think about how *you* might have felt if you had had to leave your home when you were in second grade, and live without your parents and other family members for so long. And during that time, Olga was shuffled around from house to house, never feeling as though she belonged anywhere. How would you have handled that?

When you give your presentation to the class, be sure to emphasize how the war affected *all people*. Think about the people who took Olga in. Some of them did so grudgingly, others more willingly. Their lives were upset. Olga was Jewish, but these English people did not blame her and the other Jews for all their trouble, the way some other Europeans did. Instead, they tried their best to do what was right.

Unit Outline:

Kindertransport

by Olga Levy Drucker

Day 1:

1. Assign a role to each group member:
   (a) *Secretary:* Someone to record the group assignments and discussions. In recording the discussions, the Secretary should describe the general discussion—who thought what—and then describe how the discussion ended. Was there a consensus?
   (b) *Taskmaster:* Someone to read instructions each day and keep the group on task.
   (c) *Assignment Collector:* Someone to make sure all assignments get turned in each day.
   (d) *Librarian:* Someone to get the books and return them each day. The Librarian will also complete any research required.
   (e) *Activity Director:* Someone to organize group activities.

2. Identify group members who would like to read aloud.

3. Complete the Questionnaire sheet on your own. Upon completion, discuss your responses with your group. Why did you choose the items you did? Does your group have the same or differing opinions? Justify or defend your responses on the back of your questionnaire.*

4. The Librarian needs to get the books at this point.

5. The Taskmaster will read the introductory material aloud to the group so that all group members will have a good idea of what will be expected during the unit.

6. If there's still time left in the class period, begin reading aloud.

Day 2:

1. Read Chapters 1 and 2.

2. Fill out Day 2 Section Summary/Title worksheet. This can be a group effort; however, each group member will be responsible for his/her own paper. This assignment will be turned in when you're finished reading the book.

3. This book has a lot of characters, and a character chart will help you to keep track of who is who. Make a chart of the important characters using your own paper. Include the following information:

   (a) name (you might include their relationship to the main character)
   (b) physical description (height, weight, hair color, eye color, etc.)
   (c) profession, hobbies, and interests
   (d) what they have lost or what has been taken away from them

   At the end of the unit you will be turning in a final, polished copy, so you should work on a rough draft during the reading and rewrite your chart when you have completed the novel.

---

* All group discussions must be written up by the Secretary and turned in at the completion of the discussion.

Unit Outline: *Kindertransport*

4. Group activity: Make a list of all the things mentioned in Chapter 2 that this family owned that were enjoyable, delicious, etc., or that suggest the good life. Put one copy of the list in the basket by the end of the period. Include the names of all group members.*

Day 3:
1. Read Chapter 3, and to the break on p. 23.
2. Fill out Section Summary/Title sheet for today's reading. Also add any new characters that have been introduced.
3. Group activity: Begin making a chart of some German words and expressions that appear in the book. What do the following German phrases mean? Each person needs to maintain a copy of the chart, although the group should work together on this.
   p. 9: *Schlingel*
   p. 11: *Wurstchen*
   p. 13: *Sturm Abteilung*
   p. 21: *Kristallnacht*
4. There will be more phrases in tomorrow's reading.

Day 4:
1. Read the rest of Chapter 4.
2. Fill out Section Summary/Title sheet and add to your character chart, if necessary.
3. Add to the list of German phrases from yesterday:
   p. 26: Dachau
   p. 27: (Jewish words) *Chanukah, menorah*
   p. 29: Aryan
   p. 31: *Kindertransport*
   p. 35: *Alles einsteigen*
4. Group discussion: Make a list of ways in which Hitler's movement affected Ollie's daily life. What irony begins on p. 27? Turn in one copy of the list and the answer to the question by the end of the period.*

Day 5:
1. Read Chapters 5 and 6.
2. Fill out Section Summary/Title sheet and add to your character chart, if necessary.
3. Do Colons worksheet. Each member of the group needs to turn in his/her own assignment.
4. Group discussion: Reread p. 45, first paragraph. In what ways are Ollie and the rose alike? Each group member should include the group responses at the bottom of his/ her Colon worksheet.

Day 6:
1. Read Chapters 7 and 8.
2. Fill out Section Summary/Title sheet and then add to the character chart, if necessary.
3. Individual writing assignment: Write about a time you stayed with someone or were in a strange environment where you didn't feel comfortable or at home. How did you feel? What did you do? Prepare your paper neatly and in ink. Turn in when finished.

Day 7:
1. Read Chapters 9 and 10.
2. Fill out Section Summary/Title sheet and add to the character chart, if necessary.

---

* All group discussions must be written up by the Secretary and turned in at the completion of the discussion.

Unit Outline: *Kindertransport*

3. Group discussion: From p. 75: What is implied in the expression "homefires"?*

4. Verb tense assignment: You probably have noticed that Drucker wrote this book in the past tense. To see what effect the present tense can have, rewrite paragraphs 2 through 5 on pp. 75 and 76 from today's reading in the present tense. Here is what the first paragraph sounds like in the present tense:

> The mood at boarding school is gloomy after our return. For one thing, a lot of the girls haven't come back. Some of the teachers have stayed away, too. Even June is not there anymore.

At the bottom of your assignment, write a line or two about what effect you think the present tense has on the feeling of the story. Then turn your assignment in.

Day 8:
1. Read Chapters 11 and 12.
2. Fill out Section Summary/Title sheet, and then add to the character chart, if necessary.
3. Group discussion: What is Ollie's attitude about being a Jew? What does being a Jew mean to her? (Reread her commentary on p. 81.) This time, the Secretary won't be responsible for turning in the notes; instead, each group member will record the group response to the discussion question individually.
4. Advice to the character going through the conflict. What would you say to Ollie to reassure her in her predicament? Record your own advice as well as the advice of your group. You may write on the same sheet as you used for #3. Turn in your paper.

Day 9:
1. Read Chapters 13 and 14.
2. Fill out Section Summary/Title sheet, and then add to the character chart, if necessary.

Day 10:
1. Read Chapters 15 and 16.
2. Fill out Section Summary/Title sheet, and then add to the character chart, if necessary.
3. Group discussion: p. 119—Why do you think Olga didn't seem to have any feeling? p. 122—What is Olga saying about Uncle Larry?*

Day 11:
1. Read the last two chapters of the book.
2. Finish filling out Section Summary/Title sheet and the character chart. Turn both of these assignments in today.
3. Do the Cause and Effect flowchart.
4. Assign the group Librarian to go to the library and bring back enough copies of Olga Levy Drucker's biography sheet for the class tomorrow. A good source for this information is *Something about the Author*, or another bibliographical reference set.

Day 12:
1. Read Olga Levy Drucker's biography sheet.
2. Assignment: Throughout the book, Drucker uses diamonds to separate little glimpses of Olga's life in England. Write a paper in which you tell three little stories—memories of things you have experienced. To help you think of something to write about, look at all the topics Drucker thought of and how she told each little story. Notice the lengths—some are very short, and nearly all of them include dialogue.

---

* All group discussions must be written up by the Secretary and turned in at the completion of the discussion.

Unit Outline: *Kindertransport*

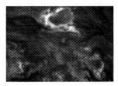

Your paper should include all three stories about your life. Get started on this assignment today, finish up tomorrow, and then turn in the final draft.

   3. Group discussion of the Importance Chart. Turn one in for the group.*

Day 13:   Begin working on the Holocaust Literature handout. The teacher will provide instructions. Use the Holocaust Essay Form for your final copy of the written assignment.

Days 14–17: 1. Holocaust essay due.

              2. Begin planning the presentation that your group will give to the class. The Taskmaster will read the instructions from the Class Presentation sheet. The group should formulate some ideas, with the Secretary taking notes. During the next four days, your group should be putting together your presentation and related assignments, as well as rehearsing for the class presentation.

                 Determine who will be responsible for what parts. Before you present, you will need to turn in a paper neatly written in ink with all of your names in the heading that will outline the responsibilities for each group member. Each member will be graded individually for his/her part in the presentation.*

Days 18–20:   Class presentations. There will be a five-question quiz at the end of each presentation.

---

* All group discussions must be written up by the Secretary and turned in at the completion of the discussion.

Name _____ Date _____

Kindertransport

by Olga Levy Drucker
Day 1: Questionnaire

Read the following questions and determine for yourself the answers you think are best. You may choose two or three items from each group.

1. *What words best describe **prejudice**?*

   _____ obstinate   _____ single-minded   _____ biased

   _____ forceful   _____ conceited   _____ ignorant

   _____ stubborn   _____ poor   _____ wealthy

   _____ judgmental   _____ unloved   _____ opinionated

2. *What do you think causes a person to become prejudiced?*

   _____ He/She was just born that way.

   _____ His/Her parents taught him/her to be that way by their example.

   _____ He/She observes incidents on television and at school.

   _____ He/She lives in an area where he/she is in the minority.

   _____ He/She lives in an area where he/she is in the vast majority.

   _____ He/She has been the victim in a race-related incident.

   _____ He/She has been the victim in an ethnic-related incident.

   _____ His/Her religion teaches supremacy of one race over another.

3. *How would you recognize a prejudiced person?*

   _____ From the way he/she lives.

   _____ From his/her facial expressions.

   _____ From his/her actions toward athletes, comedians, or politicians of different ethnic, racial, or religious backgrounds.

   _____ From the way he/she teases, taunts people.

4. *How would you cure a prejudiced person?*

   _____ With love and kindness, understanding.

   _____ With reasoning and knowledge.

   _____ By giving him/her a taste of his/her own medicine.

   _____ By getting someone to beat or frighten him/her.

   _____ There is no cure.

Holocaust Literature:
Study Guides to 12 Stories of Courage

Name _____ Date _____

Kindertransport
Summaries and Titles

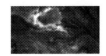

Directions:

1. Each member of the group will keep track of each of the section summaries in the book and turn in this assignment at the end of the reading. **Each of you will also be responsible for predicting future events based on what you have just read.**

2. After reading each day, look back over the pages read and think about what you might title the reading for that day if you were the author of the book. After the group members have individually decided on chapter titles, have a group discussion on why the titles were given. Which title does the group agree is the most accurate?

	Section Summary and Prediction	**Section Title**
Day 2 Pages read:		Why?
Day 3 Pages read:		Why?
Day 4 Pages read:		Why?
Day 5 Pages read:		Why?

(continued)

Kindertransport
Summaries and Titles *(continued)*

	Section Summary and Prediction	Section Title
Day 6 Pages read:		Why?
Day 7 Pages read:		Why?
Day 8 Pages read:		Why?
Day 9 Pages read:		Why?
Day 10 Pages read:		Why?
Day 11 Pages read:		Why?

Kindertransport
Day 5: Colons

A colon is a punctuation mark that is used before a long quotation, an explanation, an example, or a series. It is also used as a stylistic tool to focus the reader's attention on what is to come.

The following sentences were taken from this novel, but the colons have been replaced by commas. Insert the colons where you think they belong. Then ask your teacher for the answers so you can check your work by looking up the original sentences in the book.

1. They were prison camps where people who disagreed with Hitler were taken, communists, Gypsies, Roman Catholics, Jews, and others whom the Nazis didn't like.

2. I wondered if his eyes were looking at the terrible things that must have happened in that ghastly place. I wanted to ask him, Did they really beat you up?

3. I swallowed a lump and forced myself to think, Now I can say "the dog is under the table."

4. She might have said something like, "It isn't much, but it's home."

5. I can imagine that she might have thought, "Who is this scrawny looking brat whom my mum makes me share my room with?"

6. What I didn't know then, but have since realized, was this, if a Nazi invasion had happened, I, as a Jew—a *German* Jew at that—would have been hunted down and killed.

7. Today, a nagging voice inside me was screaming, Why? Why? Why New York?

8. Auntie Mona joined in, "This lady is Mrs. Wolton, our neighbor . . ."

Kindertransport
Day 11: Cause and Effect

Show how events in a story determine future events by filling in the squares with causes and effects from *Kindertransport*. Begin each sentence with *Since* or *Because*. When you begin a sentence with either of these two words, you create a complex sentence, and there needs to be a comma at the end of the first clause. The first one has been done for you.

Because it was dangerous for children to stay in Germany during World War II, especially Jewish children, Olga's parents sent her away in a *Kindertransport*.

Since she was sent away,

Holocaust Literature:
Study Guides to 12 Stories of Courage

Name _____ Date _____

Kindertransport
Day 12: Importance Chart

On the lines below, list the 10 events (in order of occurrence) that your group considers the most important events in the book. Then explain why.

1. _____ ,

    because _____ .

2. _____ ,

    because _____ .

3. _____ ,

    because _____ .

4. _____ ,

    because _____ .

5. _____ ,

    because _____ .

6. _____ ,

    because _____ .

7. _____ ,

    because _____ .

8. _____ ,

    because _____ .

9. _____ ,

    because _____ .

10. _____ ,

    because _____ .

Kindertransport
Grading Sheet

Assignment	Possible Points	Student ✓	Teacher ✓	Points
1. Questionnaire Responses				
2. Day 2: Group Activity				
3. Day 3: Group Activity				
4. Day 4: Group Discussion				
5. Day 5: Colons				
6. Day 5: Group Discussion				
7. Day 6: Writing Assignment				
8. Day 7: Group Discussion				
9. Day 7: Verb Tense				
10. Day 8: Discussion/Advice				
11. Day 10: Group Discussion				
12. Section Summaries/Titles				
13. Character Chart				
14. Day 11: Cause and Effect				
15. Day 12: Three Stories				
16. Day 12: Importance Chart				
17. Day 13: Holocaust Literature				
18. Day 13: Holocaust Essay				
19. Character Bag				
20. Class Presentation				
21. Class Quizzes				
22. Group Participation				
			Total Pts.	
			Grade	

Holocaust Literature:
Study Guides to 12 Stories of Courage

Touch Wood

A Girlhood in Occupied France

by Renée Roth-Hano

Touch Wood

by Renée Roth-Hano

To the Student

The book you are about to read is a true story that starts out in the eastern part of France along the German border. When Germany took over the French province of Alsace early in World War II, it was no longer safe for Renée Roth and her Jewish family to stay in their home, so they quickly moved to Paris, thinking they would be safe from the Germans there. Later, it was a shock for them to discover that the Germans would take over the entire country. In this story you will see how the war tore families apart. Renée was quite young when she and her sisters were separated from their parents.

Of all the Holocaust books in this unit, this is probably the book that best illustrates the total bewilderment of the Jewish people. This story shows how the Nazis' ideas crept into public acceptance so subtly that even neighbors who had known and liked the Roths for years suddenly began to hate and despise them.

This story is also effective at showing the effects of discrimination on one's self-esteem. Roth articulates well how it felt to wear a yellow star and how it felt to be branded "different."

The language in this book seems very simple—almost childlike. Remember when you read it that French is the author's native language, and that she wrote this book in English—it wasn't translated.

Unit Outline:

Touch Wood

by Renée Roth-Hano

Day 1:   1. Assign a role to each group member:

(a) *Secretary:* Someone to record the group assignments and discussions. In recording the discussions, the Secretary should describe the general discussion—who thought what—and then describe how the discussion ended. Was there a consensus?

(b) *Taskmaster:* Someone to read instructions each day and keep the group on task.

(c) *Assignment Collector:* Someone to make sure all assignments get turned in each day.

(d) *Librarian:* Someone to get the books and return them each day. The Librarian will also complete any research required.

(e) *Activity Director:* Someone to organize group activities.

2. Identify group members who would like to read aloud.

3. Complete the Questionnaire sheet on your own. Upon completion, discuss your responses with your group. Why did you choose the items you did? Does your group have the same or differing opinions? Justify or defend your responses on the back of your paper.*

4. The Librarian needs to get the books at this point.

5. The Taskmaster will read the introductory material aloud to the group so that all group members will have a good idea of what will be expected during the unit.

6. If there's still time left in the class period, begin reading aloud.

Day 2:   1. Read aloud to the break on p. 25.

2. Fill out Day 2 Section Summary/Title sheet. This can be a group effort; however, each group member will be responsible for his/her own paper. This assignment will be turned in when you're finished reading the book.

3. There are so many important people in the story, it's hard to keep track of them. This assignment will help. Make a chart of all the characters. Include the following information:

(a) name
(b) physical description
(c) profession or relationship to Renée
(d) what they have lost or what's been taken away from them

Do this assignment on your own paper, and it will be due when you're finished reading the book.

---

* All group discussions must be written up by the Secretary and turned in at the completion of the discussion.

            Holocaust Literature:
Study Guides to 12 Stories of Courage

Name _____ Date _____

Unit Outline: *Touch Wood*

Day 3:
1. Read aloud to the break on p. 50.
2. Fill out Section Summary/Title sheet for these pages.
3. Group discussion/research: Does anyone in the group know anything about Jewish holidays and practices? If not, go to the library to find out the importance of these holidays: Rosh Hashanah and Yom Kippur. Also find out about food restrictions for Jews. What kinds of foods can't they eat? Why? Why don't Jews celebrate Christmas? You will probably only have time to do the library research outside of class. Have the Librarian write up your group's findings and turn them in.*

Day 4:
1. Read aloud to the break on p. 73.
2. Fill out Section Summary/Title sheet.
3. Group discussion:
   (a) Several times in the book so far the author has used the expression, "touch wood" (pp. 17, 21, 48). What does this expression mean, and why did Roth-Hano use it for the title of this book? Does it fit the book so far? Why or why not?
   (b) P. 71—What does "nonassimible" mean? Why did they use such a strange word?

Day 5:
1. Read aloud to the break on p. 97.
2. Fill out Section Summary/Title sheet.
3. Tense activity. Look at the beginning of 1942 on p. 86. By now you have probably noticed that this book is written in the present tense. The present tense makes the story seem like a snapshot—never changing with time. Maybe the author is **still** experiencing these events. To see the difference that tense can make in meaning, rewrite the first part of this chapter in past tense on your own paper—to the break on p. 87. Reread the passage to yourself before turning it in, so you can see how the change in tense can change the feeling of the story. This is how you start:

   It was cold and damp, and my hands felt cold even with my gloves on, but I didn't care.

   I was in heaven.

   Today Guy commented on how he liked the plaid bow on my white shirt and the way I parted my hair . . .

   Turn in your assignment when finished.

Day 6:
1. Read aloud to the break on p. 123.
2. Fill out Section Summary/Title sheet.
3. Group discussion: What does "anti-Semitic" mean (p. 103)? Then go back over pp. 32 to 34. Here Roth-Hano provides some reasons why the Jews have been singled out to take the blame for Germany's problems. As a group, compile a list of the reasons.*

Day 7:
1. Read aloud to the break on p. 149.
2. Fill out Section Summary/Title sheet.

---

* All group discussions must be written up by the Secretary and turned in at the completion of the discussion.

Unit Outline: *Touch Wood*

3. Group discussion: Why the big fuss about the hats on p. 143? What new and strange customs and ideas do the girls encounter when they go to their first mass? The Secretary will record the information and turn it in.*

Day 8:
1. Read aloud to the bottom of p. 172.
2. Fill out Section Summary/Title sheet.

Day 9:
1. Read aloud to the break on p. 199.
2. Fill out Section Summary/Title sheet.
3. Do Colon worksheet. When you're finished, ask the teacher for the answer sheet so you can correct your work. Then answer the question at the bottom of the worksheet and turn in your assignment.

Day 10:
1. Read aloud to the break on p. 222.
2. Fill out Section Summary/Title sheet.
3. "Touch wood" or "Knock on wood" are examples of superstition: If you say something that you don't want to happen, you knock on wood to make sure it doesn't happen. Usually, we think of superstitious people as uneducated. Superstitions also don't seem to fit in with religion. Yet, as educated and often religious people, we still seem to buy into a superstition as Renée's mother did. As a group, brainstorm all the superstitions you can think of.*
4. Then each group member will choose one superstition and use it as the title of his or her story. Tell how or when you first became aware of this superstition's influence in your life. When, for example, did you first learn about stepping on a crack or Friday the 13th or breaking a mirror? Tell it like a story, and then tell how this superstition still affects you. It's not necessary for each group member to choose a different superstition.

Day 11:
1. Read aloud to the break on p. 251.
2. Do the Cause and Effect flowchart. The teacher will provide instructions.

Day 12:
1. Read aloud to the break on p. 272.
2. Fill out the Section Summary/Title sheet.

Day 13:
1. Read aloud to the end of the book.
2. Fill in the last Section Summary/Title box and turn in this assignment.
3. Discuss the Importance Chart as a group, and have the Secretary record the group consensus to turn in.*
4. Begin working on Holocaust Literature handout. The teacher will provide instructions. Use the Holocaust Essay Form for your final copy of the written assignment. You will probably have to complete this assignment at home. Turn it in two days from today.

---

* All group discussions must be written up by the Secretary and turned in at the completion of the discussion.

Unit Outline: *Touch Wood*

Days 14–17: Begin planning the presentation that will be given to the class. The Taskmaster will read the instructions from the Class Presentation sheet. The group should formulate some ideas, with the Secretary taking notes. During the next four days, your group should be putting together your presentation and related assignments, as well as rehearsing for the class presentation.

Determine who will be responsible for what parts. Before you present, you will need to turn in a paper neatly written in ink with all of your names in the heading that will outline the responsibilities for each group member. Each member will be graded individually on his/her part in the presentation.*

Days 18–20: Class presentations. There will be a five-question quiz at the end of each presentation.

---

* All group discussions must be written up by the Secretary and turned in at the completion of the discussion.

Touch Wood

by Renée Roth-Hano
Day 1: Questionnaire

Read the following questions and determine for yourself the answers you think fit best. You may choose two or three items from each group.

1. *What words best describe* **prejudice**?

   _____ obstinate   _____ single-minded   _____ biased

   _____ forceful   _____ conceited   _____ ignorant

   _____ stubborn   _____ poor   _____ wealthy

   _____ judgmental   _____ unloved   _____ opinionated

2. *What do you think causes a person to become prejudiced?*

   _____ He/She was just born that way.

   _____ His/Her parents taught him/her to be that way by their example.

   _____ He/She observes incidents on television and at school.

   _____ He/She lives in an area where he/she is in the minority.

   _____ He/She lives in an area where he/she is in the vast majority.

   _____ He/She has been the victim in a race-related incident.

   _____ He/She has been the victim in an ethnic-related incident.

   _____ His/Her religion teaches supremacy of one race over another.

3. *How would you recognize a prejudiced person?*

   _____ From the way he/she lives.

   _____ From his/her facial expressions.

   _____ From his/her actions toward athletes, comedians, or politicians of different ethnic, racial, or religious backgrounds.

   _____ From the way he/she teases, taunts people.

4. *How would you cure a prejudiced person?*

   _____ With love and kindness, understanding.

   _____ With reasoning and knowledge.

   _____ By giving him/her a taste of his/her own medicine.

   _____ By getting someone to beat or frighten him/her.

   _____ There is no cure.

Name _____ Date _____

Touch Wood
Summaries and Titles

Directions:

1. Each member of the group will keep track of each of the section summaries in the book and turn in this assignment at the end of the reading. **Each of you will also be responsible for predicting future events based on what you have just read.**

2. After reading each day, look back over the pages read and think about what you might title the reading for that day if you were the author of the book. After the group members have individually decided on chapter titles, have a group discussion on why the titles were given. Which title does the group agree is the most accurate?

	Section Summary and Prediction	**Section Title**
Day 2 Pages read:		Why?
Day 3 Pages read:		Why?
Day 4 Pages read:		Why?
Day 5 Pages read:		Why?

(continued)

Touch Wood
Summaries and Titles *(continued)*

	Section Summary and Prediction	**Section Title**
Day 6 Pages read:		Why?
Day 7 Pages read:		Why?
Day 8 Pages read:		Why?
Day 9 Pages read:		Why?
Day 10 Pages read:		Why?

Touch Wood
Summaries and Titles *(continued)*

	Section Summary and Prediction	**Section Title**
Day 11 Pages read:		Why?
Day 12 Pages read:		Why?
Day 13 Pages read:		Why?

Holocaust Literature:
Study Guides to 12 Stories of Courage

Touch Wood
Day 9: Colons

A colon is a punctuation mark that is used before a long quotation, an explanation, an example, or a series. It is also used as a stylistic tool to focus the reader's attention on what is to come. It's kind of like a ***ta da!***

The following sentences were taken from this novel, but the colons have been removed. Insert the colons where you think they belong. When you're done, ask your teacher for the answer sheet so you can check your work by looking up the original sentences in the book.

1. Our aunt is far from being so easygoing with us, in fact, she is rather bossy.

2. Maman welcomed the idea, because she is such a stickler about keeping our dresses clean.

3. I suddenly don't care about my Alsatian accent and the rest, and I know I am going to like my new school.

4. Besides, they say that you can't really trust the press, the Germans are censoring everything in the news.

5. Sometimes our laughs stop abruptly, and we think we recognize a passerby.

6. Maman is not crazy about the friendship, she never liked Papa playing cards.

7. In school, though, it is Maréchal Pétain who counts, and his picture is all over the place.

8. I am grateful about one thing, though, here at least they don't force us to wear those awful gas masks.

Why would the author choose to use colons in these sentences rather than commas, semicolons, or conjunctions?

Touch Wood
Day 11: Cause and Effect

Show how events in a story determine future events by filling in the squares with causes and effects from *Touch Wood*. Begin each sentence with *Since* or *Because*. When you begin a sentence with either of these two words, you create a complex sentence, and there needs to be a comma at the end of the first clause. The first one has been done for you.

Because the Germans have moved into Alsace and declared it part of Germany, Renée and her Jewish family move to Paris where it will be safer for them.

Since they moved to Paris,

Holocaust Literature:
Study Guides to 12 Stories of Courage

Touch Wood
Day 12: Importance Chart

On the lines below, list the 10 events (in order of occurrence) that your group considers the most important events in the book. Then explain why.

1. _____ ,

   because _____ .

2. _____ ,

   because _____ .

3. _____ ,

   because _____ .

4. _____ ,

   because _____ .

5. _____ ,

   because _____ .

6. _____ ,

   because _____ .

7. _____ ,

   because _____ .

8. _____ ,

   because _____ .

9. _____ ,

   because _____ .

10. _____ ,

    because _____ .

Name _____   Date _____

Touch Wood
Grading Sheet

Assignment	Possible Points	Student ✓	Teacher ✓	Points
1. Questionnaire Responses				
2. Day 3: Group Discussion				
3. Day 4: Group Discussion				
4. Day 5: Tense Activity				
5. Day 6: Group Discussion				
6. Day 7: Group Discussion				
7. Day 9: Colons				
8. Day 11: Cause and Effect				
9. Day 12: Importance Chart				
10. Day 13: Holocaust Literature				
11. Day 13: Holocaust Essay				
12. Section Summaries/Titles				
13. Character Chart				
14. Character Bag				
15. Class Presentation				
16. Class Quizzes				
17. Group Participation				
			Total Pts.	
			Grade	

Holocaust Literature:
Study Guides to 12 Stories of Courage

Maus I and II

A Survivor's Tale

by Art Spiegelman

Name _____   Date _____

Maus I and II

by Art Spiegelman

To the Student

The two volumes you are about to read will be like no books that you have ever read before. Instead of conveying everything in words, Art Spiegelman utilizes cartoons to help get his message across. Art chose his parents (mainly his father) as his central characters, primarily because he wanted to tell the story of their survival during World War II.

While working on these book-length comic strips, Artie spent some time with his father, Vladek, interviewing him to make the story as accurate as possible. He includes these interviews as well as Vladek's memories of the war in his cartoons so we can see how deeply Vladek was affected by the events that took place. Artie depicts his conversations with other people as well, so that you get a good idea of the challenges he encountered in creating this book.

Another interesting aspect of *Maus I* and *Maus II* is that the story takes place within two time periods. The author uses the present time period, which is the time during which he interviewed his father; and the "past-present," when we revert to Vladek and his life during World War II.

Symbolism is used heavily throughout the story to help portray both the mood and the underlying themes. Watch the animals Artie uses to depict the different characters. You will notice that the Jews are represented by mice, the Germans by cats, and the Americans by dogs. Why would he use these animals as symbols? What does this indicate?

Think about these things as you prepare for your presentation. You might also come up with a chart to help track the two different stories that alternate in these two volumes. Keep the plot summaries as simple as you can. It would be easy to confuse the two different stories, thus confusing your audience as well.

Name _____   Date _____

Unit Outline:

Maus I and *Maus II*

by Art Spiegelman

Day 1:

1. Assign a role to each group member:

   (a) *Secretary:* Someone to record the group assignments and discussions. In recording the discussions, the Secretary should describe the general discussion—who thought what—and then describe how the discussion ended. Was there a consensus?

   (b) *Taskmaster:* Someone to read instructions each day and keep the group on task.

   (c) *Assignment Collector:* Someone to collect assignments and turn them in each day.

   (d) *Librarian:* Someone to get the books and return them each day. The Librarian will also complete any research required.

   (e) *Activity Director:* Someone to organize group activities.

2. Identify group members who would like to read aloud.

3. Complete the Questionnaire sheet on your own. Upon completion, discuss your responses with your group. Why did you choose the items you did? Does your group have the same or differing opinions? Justify or defend your responses.*

4. The Librarian needs to collect the books for group members.

5. The Taskmaster will read the introductory material aloud to the group so that all group members will have a good idea of what will be expected during the unit.

6. If there's still time left in the class period, browse through your books. Discuss and predict what you think this book will be like.

Day 2:

1. Look up "symbolism" in the dictionary and any other reference book you have access to. Have the Secretary record the meaning on paper. Have each group member come up with at least two examples of symbolism we see every day in our world. Record the examples on the same paper, identifying who said what.*

2. Now look at the cover of *Maus I*. Record any examples of symbolism you see on the cover.*

3. Have the Librarian look up "flashback" in the dictionary and/or any reference book you have access to. Write down the definition on today's group discussion page. Discuss the meaning of "flashback" and make sure everyone in your group understands the term.* *Maus I* and *Maus II* use flashbacks quite a bit, and the stories can often get confusing. It is important that everyone understands the purpose of flashbacks and how they can be used.

4. Group discussion: Discuss the title of these books. Why would Art Spiegelman choose this title? What about the spelling: "Maus"? Record possible reasons on your group discussion paper. Look also at the *Maus I* subtitle, "My Father Bleeds History." Predict what this may mean.*

5. Turn to p. 4. Read the quote and dedication aloud.

---

* All group discussions must be written up by the Secretary and turned in at the completion of the discussion.

Unit Outline: *Maus I* and *Maus II*

6. Begin reading *Maus I* aloud. It is very important that this whole book be read aloud so that everyone can understand what is going on. Art Spiegelman uses symbolism and flashback throughout both volumes. You must be aware of these devices and pick up on the different parts to understand what is happening.

There are a couple of options for reading this aloud. You can assign characters and read parts, or you can take turns reading chapters. It might help to change voices for the different characters so it doesn't get confusing.

Day 3:

1. Read through Chapter 1 aloud (p. 23).

2. Fill out Day 3 Section Summary/Title sheet. Make sure you read the directions carefully. This can be a group effort; however, each group member will be responsible for his/her own paper. This assignment will be turned in when you are finished reading the book.*

3. This book has a lot of characters, and a character chart will help you to keep track of who is who. Make a chart of the important characters using your own paper. Include the following information:

   (a) name (you might include their relationship to the main character)
   (b) physical description (height, weight, hair color, eye color, etc.)
   (c) profession, hobbies, and interests
   (d) what they have lost or what has been taken away from them

At the end of this unit you will be turning in a final, polished copy, so you should work on a rough draft during the reading and rewrite your chart when you have completed the novel.

Day 4:

1. Read pp. 25–59.

2. Complete Section Summary/Title worksheet.

3. Add to character chart if necessary.

4. Each group member will be responsible for a Symbolism/Observations chart. Fill in this chart as you read. Discuss any new findings as you come across them or at the end of the class period. This will help group members with understanding the plot.

Day 5:

1. Read pp. 60–93.

2. Complete Section Summary/Title worksheet.

3. Add to character chart if necessary.

4. Discuss your Symbolism/Observation worksheet, telling each other anything that you have added. These discussions do not have to be written up; however, by discussing this sheet at the end of each day, each member will be adding to their own worksheet as well as helping everyone understand what is happening.

Day 6:

1. Read pp. 95–127. Pay close attention as you are reading the comic strip "Prisoner on the Hell Planet." This contains many examples of symbolism.

2. Complete Section Summary/Title worksheet.

---

* All group discussions must be written up by the Secretary and turned in at the completion of the discussion.

Unit Outline: *Maus I* and *Maus II*

    3. Add to character chart if necessary.

    4. Discuss your Symbolism/Observation worksheet, telling each other anything that you have added.

Day 7:
    1. Read from pp. 129–159 end.

    2. Fill out Section Summary/Title worksheet.

    3. Discuss your Symbolism/Observation worksheet, telling each other anything that you have added.

Day 8:
    1. Begin reading *Maus II: And Here My Troubles Began.* Again, read the dedications on pp. 2, 3, and 5. Interpret the meanings and/or the reasons Artie put them in this book. Read the brief plot summary on p. 6. Would you add or change anything?*

    2. Read from pp. 11–22. As a group, discuss what is going on here. Make sure every group member knows what is happening.

    3. Complete Section Summary/Title worksheet.

    4. Add to your character sheet.

    5. Discuss your Symbolism/Observation worksheet, telling each other anything that you have added.

    6. Think of a time when you experienced some type of conflict. It might have been a problem with a friend, parents, or siblings. Create a personal cartoon depicting the sequence of events that lead up to that conflict, the conflict itself, and how it was resolved. You might choose to draw animals like Artie did to symbolize each character's personality. Try to use symbolism in your cartoon wherever you can. Your ideas and creativity are what will count, not your drawing ability.

Day 9:
    1. Read pp. 23–74.

    2. Complete Section Summary/Title worksheet.

    3. Add to your character sheet if necessary.

    4. Discuss your Symbolism/Observation worksheet, telling each other anything that you have added.

Day 10:
    1. Read pp. 75–100.

    2. Complete Section Summary/Title worksheet.

    3. Add to your character sheet if necessary.

    4. Discuss your Symbolism/Observation worksheet, telling each other anything that you have added.

Day 11:
    1. Read pp. 101–136 end.

    2. Complete Section Summary/Title worksheet.

    3. Add to your character sheet if necessary.

    4. Discuss your Symbolism/Observation worksheet, telling each other anything that you have added.

* All group discussions must be written up by the Secretary and turned in at the completion of the discussion.

Unit Outline: *Maus I* and *Maus II*

5. Group discussion: As a group, discuss the end of the book. Did it end as you thought it would? What do you think happened to Artie mentally? Mala? Why do you suppose Artie chose to write this in comic strip form rather than in the usual story form with words? Do you think it would have been just as good? Why or why not?

6. Complete Cause and Effect flowchart. The teacher will provide instructions. Turn in when finished.

Day 12:   1. As a group, complete the Importance Chart. You may use your section summary sheet or your observation list to help you. Complete your final copy of your character chart. This is due at the end of Day 13.

2. Essay assignment. Read the directions on the *Maus I* and *Maus II* Essay sheet. Put some time and effort into this paper as it will be worth a lot of points. This assignment is due at the end of Day 14.

Day 13:   1. Begin working on Holocaust Literature handout. The teacher will provide instructions. Use the Holocaust Essay Form for your final copy of the written assignment.

2. Work on any unfinished assignments.

3. Turn in character chart and Section Summary/Title worksheet. Make sure they are complete, with your name showing.

Days 14–17:   1. Turn in your *Maus I* and *Maus II* essay. Turn in your Symbolism/Observations worksheet as well.

2. The Taskmaster will read the instructions from the Class Presentation sheet. The group should formulate some ideas, with the Secretary taking notes. During these days, your group should be putting together your presentation and related assignments, as well as rehearsing for the class presentation.

Determine who will be responsible for what parts. Before you present, you will need to turn in a paper neatly written in ink with all of your names in the heading that will outline the responsibilities for each group member. Each member will be graded individually on his/her part in the presentation.*

Days 18–20:   Class presentations. There will be a five-question quiz at the end of each presentation.

---

* All group discussions must be written up by the Secretary and turned in at the completion of the discussion.

Name _____ Date _____

Maus I and Maus II

by Art Spiegelman
Day 1: Questionnaire

Read the following questions and determine for yourself the answers you think fit best. You may choose two or three items per question.

1. *What words best describe **prejudice**?*

   _____ obstinate   _____ single-minded   _____ biased

   _____ forceful   _____ conceited   _____ ignorant

   _____ stubborn   _____ poor   _____ wealthy

   _____ judgmental   _____ unloved   _____ opinionated

2. *What do you think causes a person to become prejudiced?*

   _____ He/She was just born that way.

   _____ His/Her parents taught him/her to be that way by their example.

   _____ He/She observes incidents on television and at school.

   _____ He/She lives in an area where he/she is in the minority.

   _____ He/She lives in an area where he/she is in the vast majority.

   _____ He/She has been the victim in a race-related incident.

   _____ He/She has been the victim in an ethnic-related incident.

   _____ His/Her religion teaches supremacy of one race over another.

3. *How would you recognize a prejudiced person?*

   _____ From the way he/she lives.

   _____ From his/her facial expressions.

   _____ From his/her actions toward athletes, comedians, or politicians of different ethnic, racial, or religious backgrounds.

   _____ From the way he/she teases, taunts people.

4. *How would you cure a prejudiced person?*

   _____ With love and kindness, understanding.

   _____ With reasoning and knowledge.

   _____ By giving him/her a taste of his/her own medicine.

   _____ By getting someone to beat or frighten him/her.

   _____ There is no cure.

Holocaust Literature:
Study Guides to 12 Stories of Courage

Maus I and *Maus II*
Summaries and Titles

Directions:

1. Each member of the group will keep track of each of the section summaries in the book and turn in this assignment at the end of the reading. **Each of you will also be responsible for predicting future events based on what you have just read.**

2. After reading each day, look back over the pages read and think about what you might title the reading for that day if you were the author of the book. After the group members have individually decided on chapter titles, have a group discussion on why the titles were given. Which title does the group agree is the most accurate?

	Section Summary and Prediction	Section Title
Day 2 Pages read:		Why?
Day 3 Pages read:		Why?
Day 4 Pages read:		Why?
Day 5 Pages read:		Why?

(continued)

Maus I and *Maus II*
Summaries and Titles *(continued)*

	Section Summary and Prediction	Section Title
Day 6 Pages read:		Why?
Day 7 Pages read:		Why?
Day 8 Pages read:		Why?
Day 9 Pages read:		Why?
Day 10 Pages read:		Why?

(continued)

Holocaust Literature:
Study Guides to 12 Stories of Courage

Maus I and *Maus II*
Summaries and Titles *(continued)*

	Section Summary and Prediction	Section Title
Day 11 Pages read:		Why?
Day 12 Pages read:		Why?

Name _____   Date _____

Maus I
Day 4: Symbolism/Observations

In the Symbolism column below, list any examples of symbolism you see as you are reading the comic strip. Record the page number as well. In the Observations column, list anything that might help you to understand the story better. The first couple have been done for you.

Examples of Symbolism	Page	Observations	Page
—Jews are drawn as mice.	whole book	—Vladek has a thing about wooden hangers.	11
—Train ticket symbolizes traveling a lot.	15	—Vladek has a number tattooed on his arm (75113).	12

Holocaust Literature:
Study Guides to 12 Stories of Courage

Maus II
Day 8: Symbolism/Observations

In the Symbolism column below, list any examples of symbolism you see as you are reading the comic strip. Record the page number as well. In the Observations column, list anything that might help you to understand the story better.

Examples of Symbolism	Page	Observations	Page

Holocaust Literature:
Study Guides to 12 Stories of Courage

Maus I and *Maus II*
Day 11: Cause and Effect

Show how events in a story determine future events by filling in the squares with causes and effects from the "present-day" story in *Maus I* and *Maus II*. Begin each sentence with *Since* or *Because*. When you begin a sentence with either of these two words, you create a complex sentence, and there needs to be a comma at the end of the first clause. The first one has been done for you.

Because Artie Spiegelman wanted to know why his father acted strangely, he decided to write a comic strip based on his father's life during World War II.

Since Artie decided to write the comic strip,

Holocaust Literature:
Study Guides to 12 Stories of Courage

Maus I and *Maus II*
Day 11: Cause and Effect

Show how events in a story determine future events by filling in the squares with causes and effects from the World War II story in *Maus I* and *Maus II*. Begin each sentence with *Since* or *Because*. When you begin a sentence with either of these two words, you create a complex sentence, and there needs to be a comma at the end of the first clause. The first one has been done for you.

Since Vladek Spiegelman was Jewish, he and his friends became very nervous when the Nazis invaded Poland.

Because Vladek and his friends were nervous when the Nazis invaded Poland,

Holocaust Literature:
Study Guides to 12 Stories of Courage

Name _____   Date _____

Maus I and *Maus II*
Day 12: *Maus* Essay

Write an essay on **one** of the following topics. You may use the books and/ or any of the worksheets you have been working on to help you. Some of your theories may be speculation (guessing); that is great as long as you use specific examples to support your ideas.

Be sure to include an introduction, supporting paragraphs (be as specific as possible), and a conclusion. When finished, turn in your final copy with your rough draft.

1. Using specific examples, explain the significance of the symbolism used throughout the story, i.e., how was it used? How did it help in understanding the story?

2. Using specific examples, describe the effects the war had on both Vladek and Artie. Make sure you explain where these effects started.

3. In your opinion, why did Artie feel the need to document his father's life through a comic strip? Use examples to support your theories.

4. Write a book review for *Maus I* and *Maus II*. Be sure to include your opinions. If you recommend the books, explain why. If you do not, you must also explain why.

5. Discuss the different animals used to represent the characters. What is the significance? Describe each one and explain why that particular animal may have been chosen.

6. What was *Maus* all about? Why the animals? What are some of the other ways Artie used symbolism to make his point? Why do you think the author used the present-time story in addition to the World War II story?

Holocaust Literature:
Study Guides to 12 Stories of Courage

Name _____ Date _____

Maus I and *Maus II*
Grading Sheet

Assignment	Possible Points	Student ✓	Teacher ✓	Points
1. Questionnaire Responses				
2. Day 2: Group Discussion				
3. Day 8: Group Discussion				
4. Day 11: Group Discussion				
5. Day 11: Cause and Effect (A)				
6. Day 11: Cause and Effect (B)				
7. Day 12: Importance Chart				
8. Personal Comic Strip				
9. Character Chart				
10. Section Summaries/Titles				
11. *Maus* Essay				
12. Day 13: Holocaust Literature				
13. Day 13: Holocaust Essay				
14. Symbolism/Observation				
15. Character Bag				
16. Class Presentation				
17. Class Quizzes				
18. Group Participation				
			Total Pts.	
			Grade	

Holocaust Literature:
Study Guides to 12 Stories of Courage

Appendix

Class Presentation

Each group will prepare a half-day presentation of their story to the class. The presentation will need to include these parts:

1. Set the scene and introduce the book.
2. Tell the story to the class.
3. Present the character bag to the class, explaining the outside and inside of the character.
4. Explain the value of the book.
5. Answer student and teacher questions.
6. Give a quiz.

Set the scene:

Give the title of the book and the name of the author. Then explain where your story takes place and who the main characters are. To keep from boring the audience, make this part creative. You might show a map of the area, create a chart of the characters (using poster board or construction paper), act out some parts, etc. This part of the presentation should include something for the rest of the class to look at (something visual) so the other students can relate better to the story.

Tell the story:

The Importance Chart that the group made will help focus the telling so the story doesn't get too complicated. Each group member will tell part of the story, so if there are five group members, then there should be five parts of the story to tell. Do **not** use the Importance Chart as a visual aid or even to read from. It is simply to help you get your thoughts in order.

Present the character bag:

The purpose of a character bag is to show what the main character is like on the outside and on the inside.

On the outside of a paper grocery bag, paste pictures and words that represent the side of the character that he or she presents to the world. For example, the pictures and words might show the character's physical traits, hobbies, interests, actions, language, and visible feelings.

On the inside of the bag, paste pictures and words that represent the side of the character that he or she does **not** show the world. For example, the pictures and words might show the character's inner traits, thoughts, feelings, and secrets. You should also fill the bag with items that represent or symbolize anything about the character.

Choose the person or people who will present the character bag to the class.

You don't need to explain every single item on or in the bag; instead, you can group the items into categories. For example, when you discuss the character's personality, you can list the items on or in the bag that are personality traits. Some items will need more explanation than others. *Be aware that some of the information that comes from the character bag might require further explanation of what happened in the story.*

Value of the book:

Explain what new things your group learned about the war, about people, and about themselves while reading this book. Does the group recommend it to the rest of the class for reading? Why or why not?

Questions:

Provide time to answer questions from the class.

Class Presentation

Quiz:

Have a five-question comprehension quiz prepared to give to the class. Your group will be responsible for grading the quizzes and returning them to the other students.

Suggestions:

1. The main thing to keep in mind when you plan your presentation is to be creative. Present the main ideas of your book in such a way that the other students will get involved in what you have to share with them. Avoid simply standing in front of the room and *telling* the story. The more variety in your presentation, the better.

2. Be sure to emphasize the information that will be on the quiz at the end. Don't quiz students on little details that are hard to pick out.

3. The more visual aids, the better. Use charts and pictures (and your character bag, of course). You can also bring props to help others visualize the story better.

4. As for the format of the presentation, here are some possibilities:

   (a) Prepare a radio interview with one of the characters in the book.
   (b) Do a skit or some kind of physical representation of the main idea you want to convey to the class.
   (c) Involve the students in brainstorming ideas on a topic.
   (d) Act out a part of the book.
   (e) Play music that represents an important part of the story.
   (f) Read a section from the book that you especially liked or that shows the true meaning of the book.
   (g) Show a short part of a video to help the students visualize an idea in the book.

5. The class might be very interested to find out what has become of the author. Is he/she still alive? If so, where does he or she live? Do some research in the library to find this and other information about the author.

Day 13: Holocaust Literature

Idea	What happened in the book?	When have you experienced this?
Fear		
Inhumanity to man		
Survival/Motivation to live		
Human breaking point		
Change in needs or values		
Liberation		
Realization of what's happening		

Writing assignment

Choose **one** of the following assignments to turn in. Your final copy should be written on the Holocaust Essay Form provided.

1. Choose your most powerful memory from the last column and write about it in one of the following forms:
   (a) essay
   (b) story
2. Use all of the information in the last column to create a poem in free verse—no rhyming.

Holocaust Literature:
Study Guides to 12 Stories of Courage

Name _____ Date _____

Holocaust Essay Form

Assignment: _____

_____

_____

_____

_____

_____

_____

_____

_____

_____

_____

_____

_____

_____

_____

_____

_____

_____

_____

_____

_____

_____

_____

_____

_____

_____

(continued)

Name _____ Date _____

Assignment: _____

_____

_____

_____

_____

_____

_____

_____

_____

_____

_____

_____

_____

_____

_____

_____

_____

_____

_____

_____

_____

_____

_____

_____

_____

_____

_____

Name _____ Date _____

Group Presentation Evaluation

Book: _____

Group Members: _____ _____

_____ _____ _____

1. Introduction of the book, with background information:

2. Story summary:

3. Character bag:

4. Value of the book:

5. Questions and quiz:

   Creativity:

   Clarity and Organization:

   Group demonstrated understanding of the book:

Additional comments on back

Name _____ Date _____

Quiz Grades

Book Name _____

   1. _____

   2. _____

   3. _____

   4. _____

   5. _____

SCORE [ ]

Book Name _____

   1. _____

   2. _____

   3. _____

   4. _____

   5. _____

SCORE [ ]

Book Name _____

   1. _____

   2. _____

   3. _____

   4. _____

   5. _____

SCORE [ ]

Holocaust Unit Evaluation

1. Knowing the work involved in the unit (worksheets, group discussions, etc.), what would you change or get rid of altogether? Why?

2. What were the best and worst parts of the unit?

3. Was it helpful to work with a group? If so, explain why. If not, suggest a better arrangement.

4. Was the unit too long or too short? Did you need more time to read the book or prepare for the presentations? Be specific.

5. Which group had the best presentation and why? Which of the other books would you like to read? List them in order of preference.

6. What was the most valuable lesson or idea that you learned from the *entire* Holocaust unit?

Answer Sheets

I Am Fifteen—And I Don't Want to Die!

Semicolon Answer Sheet

1. p. 28
2. p. 29
3. p. 51
4. p. 51
5. p. 74
6. p. 75
7. p. 76

Figurative Language Answer Sheet

1. personification
2. irony
3. simile
4. irony

5. simile
6. personification
7. irony
8. simile

Colon Answer Sheet

1. p. 14
2. p. 27
3. p. 89
4. p. 90
5. p. 98
6. p. 100
7. p. 118
8. p. 120

Night

Dialogue Answer Sheet

"Here, kid, how old are you?"

It was one of the prisoners who asked me this. I could not see his face, but his voice was tense and weary.

"I'm not quite fifteen yet."

"No, eighteen."

"But I'm not," I said. "Fifteen."

"Fool. Listen to what I say."

Then he questioned my father, who replied: "Fifty."

The other grew more furious than ever.

"No, not fifty. Forty. Do you understand? Eighteen and forty."

The Hiding Place

Dialogue Answer Sheet

"Miss ten Boom," he said. "Welcome."

"How do you do, Sir."

The chief had left his desk to shut the door behind me. "Do sit down," he said. "I know all about you, you know. About your work."

"The watchmaking you mean. You're probably thinking more about my father's work than my own."

The chief smiled. "No, I mean your other work."

"Ah, then you're referring to my work with retarded children? Yes. Let me tell you about that—."

"No, Miss ten Boom," the chief lowered his voice. "I am not talking about your work with retarded children. I'm talking about still another work, and I want you to know that some of us here are in sympathy."

The chief was smiling broadly now. Tentatively I smiled back. "Now, Miss ten Boom," he went on, "I have a request."

The chief sat down on the edge of his desk and looked at me steadily. He dropped his voice until it was just audible. He was, he said, working with the underground himself. But an informer in the police department was leaking information to the Gestapo. "There's no way for us to deal with this man but to kill him."

Punctuation Answer Sheet

I tried again to protest, but Mr. Smit had forgotten I existed. Over the next few days he and his workmen were in and out of our house constantly. They never knocked. At each visit each man carried in something. Tools in a folded newspaper, a few bricks in a briefcase. "Wood!" he exclaimed when I ventured to wonder if a wooden wall would not be easier to build. "Wood sounds hollow. Hear it in a minute. No, no. Brick's the only thing for false walls."

Mischling, Second Degree

Colon Answer Sheet

1. p. 101
2. p. 131
3. p. 137
4. p. 139
5. p. 149
6. p. 158
7. p. 159
8. p. 198
9. p. 213–214
10. p. 223

Dialogue Answer Sheet

Turn to p. 117 and compare your punctuation and paragraphing with those in the book. Make any corrections you need to make.

In the Mouth of the Wolf

Figurative Language Answer Sheet

1. simile
2. irony
3. metaphor
4. metaphor
5. irony
6. simile
7. metaphor
8. simile

Colon Answer Sheet

1. p. 25
2. p. 38
3. p. 52
4. p. 61
5. p. 72
6. p. 82
7. p. 128
8. p. 142
9. p. 145
10. p. 147

Kindertransport

Colon Answer Sheet

1. p. 26
2. p. 30
3. p. 43
4. p. 45
5. p. 49
6. p. 99
7. p. 109
8. p. 131

Touch Wood

Colon Answer Sheet

1. p. 21
2. p. 29
3. p. 35
4. p. 36
5. p. 38
6. p. 41
7. p. 44
8. p. 46